❖ THE ❖
COUNTRY MUSIC
COOKBOOK

PERSONAL FAVORITE RECIPES OF COUNTRY MUSIC'S GREATEST STARS

By Dick & Sandy St. John

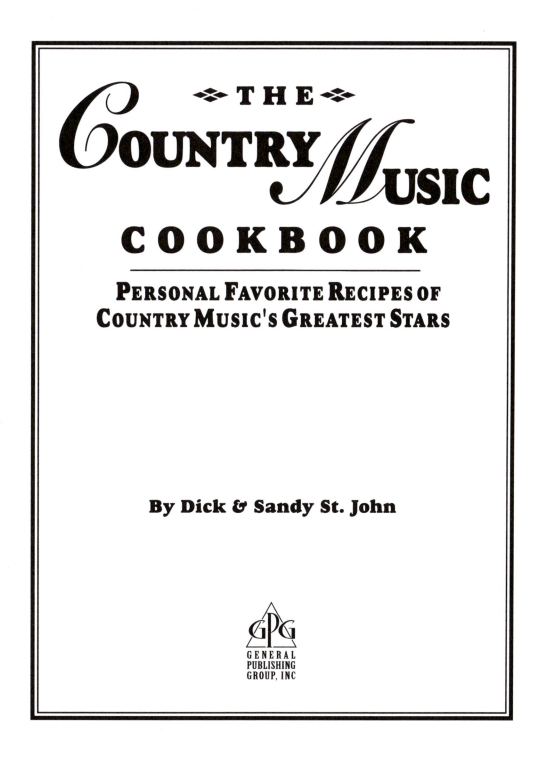

GPG
GENERAL
PUBLISHING
GROUP, INC

The publisher and authors wish to thank the following people for their contributions to the book: Corinne Baldassano, Hilary Bein, Jimmy Bowen, Sarah Brosmer, Susan Collier, Christian de Walden, Donna Fargo, Al Gallico, Bruce Greenburg, Kathy Gurley, Monika Henreid, Bruce Hinton, Howard Houck, Tim Kehr, Margo Leavin, Diane McCall, Paul Petersen, Gerard Purcell, Chuck and Marcia Rubin, Deborah Stone, Joan and Cliffie Stone, Margot and Jim Wagner and Jill Wylly.

Special thanks to our friend Ed Salamon for his invaluable assistance. And to Ron Wolfson for sharing pictures from his vast collection of country music photographs...thank you!

Very special thanks to the artists, managers, agents, chefs and relatives for their generous contributions to this special project and for their genuine concern for their fellow music industry professionals.

The National Music Foundation:
Dick Clark, Chairman of the Board
Gloria Pennington, President and CEO
Call 1-800-USA-MUSIC for more information

Front cover photo © Tony Stone Worldwide

Publisher: W. Quay Hays
Managing Editor: Sarah Pirch
Designer: Sheryl Winter
Production Director: Nadeen Torio
Copy Editor: Charles Neighbors

Library of Congress Catalog Card Number: 94-77845
ISBN 1-881649-38-5: $19.99

10 9 8 7 6 5 4 3 2 1

Printed in the U.S.A.

Contents

THE NATIONAL MUSIC FOUNDATION
MISSION STATEMENT

The National Music Foundation is a not-for-profit organization dedicated to American music and the people who bring it to us. Our mission is twofold:

1. To educate the public about American music in order to preserve our nation's musical heritage;

2. To provide for the retirement of professionals from the fields of music, radio and recording, with provisions made for those who can't afford to retire on their own.

We will fulfill this mission through The National Music Center.

The National Music Center's educational facilities will include an interactive museum, performance centers, a library and archive, a radio broadcast facility and recording studio. The Center will present workshops and classes in all forms, styles and genres of American music. Through scholarships, grants and mentor programs, the Center will encourage students to pursue studies of American music at all educational levels.

The Center will include a residence where professionals from music, radio and recording can retire among their peers and provide a core faculty for the Center's educational and mentor programs

We believe that American music, in its endless variety, is an important element in the national heritage of every citizen.

INTRODUCTION

There has never been, in the history of country music, a book quite like this one. *The Country Music Cookbook* brings together some of the greatest stars of country music and some of their favorite foods. By purchasing it, you not only acquire a collection of great recipes, but also benefit The National Music Foundation, an organization to preserve our nation's musical heritage and provide for the retirement of professionals from the fields of music, radio and recording. I'm proud to serve on their national Board of Directors.

Although you may not recognize my name, you are probably familiar with my work if you listen to country radio. I've created and produced some of radio's most successful weekly programs, including "The Weekly Country Music Countdown," "Country Gold Saturday Night," "90's Country" and "Acoustic Country," and dozens of specials including the *Billboard* award-winning "Johnny Cash Silver Anniversary Special." I also oversee Westwood One Radio Networks' seven 24-hour formats, two of which are country and am in my second term as President of the Country Radio Broadcasters. I was honored to be chosen to head the list of the "Most Influential Country Programmers of All Time," published by *Radio & Records*.

I'm very happy that so many of my friends and colleagues have been kind enough to help this project by donating the secrets of their personal favorite recipes. A look at the contributors shows that this book features the greatest collection of country music stars ever assembled. And if it's true that you are what you eat, this book says lots about the world of country music.

On behalf of the National Music Foundation, I would like to thank Dick and Sandy St. John for making this book possible.

Now, chow down!

ED SALAMON
President, Westwood One Radio Networks

FOREWORD

In the late 50s and early 60s, "Top 40" radio was much more undiversified than it is today. All the "rock and roll" stations played basically the same songs, and the hits of the day wove quite a musical tapestry. You could listen to your number-one local station for an hour and hear Patsy Cline, Marty Robbins and Conway Twitty right along with the Shirelles, Freddy Cannon and Little Eva. Neil Sedaka's "Breakin' Up Is Hard To Do" could be heard back-to-back with "Wolverton Mountain" by Claude King. Maybe that's why, in the 90s, doing "rock and roll" oldies shows performing as "Dick and Dee Dee," we have worked with country artists here in this cookbook like Sue Thompson, Freddy Fender and Dickey Lee. But we first remember country music as little children growing up in Los Angeles. Television shows like "Hometown Jamboree," "Town Hall Party" and "The Spade Cooley Show" were never missed in our homes. We both even remember going to a "Town Hall Party" picnic or two with our families.

We have been involved with the National Music Foundation since 1988. Last year we wrote *The Rock & Roll Cookbook* to benefit the NMF, and it seemed only natural to follow it up with *The Country Music Cookbook*. We've always felt that the music industry should have a home where singers, songwriters and musicians could retire if they were in need. The film industry takes care of its own with the Motion Picture Home, and it only makes sense for the music industry to do the same. That's why we decided to create these cookbooks. It is a fact that in the 50s and 60s many recording artists didn't get paid properly. As a result of this, too many beloved entertainers who were the roots of American music have died penniless or live in poverty even though their records continue to be played around the world every day. It was a great experience putting this book together and we cheered as each recipe came in from all the good and caring people who contributed.

We thank Father/Mother God for bringing this idea into fruition and dedicate this book to the future of The National Music Foundation and to the pioneers of country music who have already graduated from this school of life. God bless you all.

DICK & SANDY ST. JOHN

Conversion Table for Weight Measurements (Approximate)

OUNCES TO GRAMS

Ounces	Grams	Ounces	Grams
1	28	4	113
1 ½	43	4 ½	128
2	57	5	142
2 ½	71	5 ½	156
3	85	6	170
3 ½	99		

Conversion Table for Volume Measurements

TEASPOONS TO MILLILITERS

tsp	ml
½	2.5
1	5.0
1 ½	7.5
2	10.0
2 ½	12.5
3	15.0

TEASPOONS TO TABLESPOONS

tsp	Tbsp
1	⅓
2	⅔
3	1
6	2
9	3

TABLESPOONS TO MILLILITERS

Tbsp	ml	Tbsp	ml
½	7.5	2 ½	37.5
1	15.0	3	45.0
1 ½	22.5	3 ½	52.5
2	30.0	4	60.0

QUARTS TO LITERS

quarts	liters	quarts	liters
1	1.0	3	3.0
1½	1.5	3½	3.5
2	2.0	4 (or	4.0
2½	2.5	1 gallon)	

OVEN TEMPERATURE CHART

Recipe Calls For:	Fahrenheit Degrees	Centigrade Degrees
Warm	200–225	93–107
Very Low	250–275	121–135
Low	300–325	149–163
Medium	350–375	177–191
High	400–425	204–218
Very High	450–475	232–246
Extremely High	500–525	260–274
Broil	600	316

Formula for converting from Fahrenheit to Centigrade:
  Start with °F temperature,
  Subtract 32,
  Multiply by 5,
  Divide by 9,
Result is °C temperature equivalent.

Formula for converting from Centigrade to Fahrenheit:
  Start with °C temperature,
  Multiply by 9,
  Divide by 5,
  Add 32,
Result is °F temperature equivalent.

ABBREVIATIONS FOR MEASURING UNITS

Unit Name	Symbol	Unit Name	Symbol
Centigrade, degree	°C	meter	m
centimeter	cm	milligram	mg
Fahrenheit, degree	°F	milliliter	ml
gram	g	ounce	oz
inch	in	pint, liquid	pt
kilogram	kg	pound	lb
liter	liter	quart, liquid	qt
		tablespoon	Tbsp
		teaspoon	tsp

11

Relishes, Preserves & Condiments

LYNN ANDERSON

Born in Grand Forks, North Dakota, Lynn Anderson was raised in California. Lynn is the daughter of songwriting great Liz Anderson who composed hits such as "The Fugitive" and "My Friends Are Gonna Be Strangers" for Merle Haggard. (Merle named his band The Strangers after the latter hit.) By the time Lynn turned twenty, she had been with a national recording company for three years and was a regular on Lawrence Welk's TV show.

In 1970, she moved to Nashville and began turning out a steady stream of well received records, including "I've Been Everywhere," "Promises, Promises," "Big Girls Don't Cry" and her huge hit "Rocky Top." But it was the Joe South song "I Never Promised You A Rose Garden" that transformed the young singer into a national celebrity. The album of the same title (produced by Glenn Sutton) earned Lynn sixteen gold albums worldwide, won her a Grammy for Best Vocal Performance of the Year and the Academy of Country Music's Best Female Artist. She has sung for three presidents and the Queen of England and was named Female Country Artist of the Decade by *Record World*.

Lynn is a champion horsewoman; she won the 1987 Celebrity Cutting Competition held in Fort Worth, Texas, and participated in the Horse Fair at Belmont Stakes in 1988. In 1992, she won the Hawaiian Invitational Cutting Competition in Kamuela. She is the founder of Special Riders of Animaland, a horseback riding therapy program which teaches handicapped children to ride horses for physical and emotional therapy.

Lynn's new album is *Cowboy's Sweetheart*, a collection of songs reflecting her love of the American West. Emmylou Harris and Marty Stuart are guest performers.

NACHO MAMA'S SALSA

[16 oz recipe]

12 oz canned whole tomatoes (fresh if
    in season)
¾ oz anaheim peppers
½ oz jalapeño peppers

1½ oz white onion
¼ oz fresh garlic
1 cup cilantro

Chop all ingredients and mix well.

BOXCAR WILLIE

BoxCar Willie has fifteen gold albums and four platinum albums to his credit. One would think that he'd been performing all his life, when, in fact, it was in 1976 that he gambled it all on his hobo character. Today he is proud to be the 60th member inducted into the Grand Ole Opry and the recipient of a Bronze Star in Country Music's Hall of Fame Walkway of the Stars.

A 22-year veteran of the United States Air Force, BoxCar Willie was born in Sterrett, Texas. Being reared on country music, freight trains and hobos had a definite effect on him. With a railroad man as the head of the household and a train yard for a backyard, he learned a lot about train hobos with their tall tales and vagabond lifestyles. When he was two years old, he began imitating the train whistles and would spend evenings listening to his father play the fiddle, passing along music rich in Tennessee ancestry.

His first TV record album, *King of the Road*, sold more than three million copies, insuring BoxCar Willie international stardom. He makes over 250 personal appearances a year in the United States, Ireland, Germany, Sweden, Norway, Canada, England and Australia. In 1987, he opened a theatre in Branson, Missouri, and in 1990 opened a museum next door that features his airplane and railroad collection, as well as many items donated by friends, fans and other entertainers. In 1993, two BoxCar Willie Motels were built behind the theatre.

THE FAVORITE HOBO'S FAVORITE PEACH HONEY BUTTER

18 medium-sized ripe peaches, washed
   and peeled
¼ cup water

2¼ cups sugar
¾ cup honey

Chop peaches coarsely. Cook until soft. Press through colander or food press or use a food processor. Put 6 cups pulp in large pan. Stir in sugar and honey. Heat to boiling, stirring constantly, for 40 – 50 minutes. Place pan in ice water bath for 10 minutes.

DAVID ALLAN COE

Early in his singing career, back in the late 60s, David Allan Coe took to the stage as a masked man. He billed himself as the Mysterious Rhinestone Cowboy and no one knew his real name. "Nobody knew what I looked like," he says, "but what I looked like didn't matter. It was the music that counted." As a songwriter, his first big break came in 1973, when Tanya Tucker had a hit with his song "Would You Lay With Me (In A Field Of Stone)."

A year later, he wrote the Johnny Paycheck smash hit "Take This Job And Shove It." It was in 1975 that he had his first big hit as a recording artist with "You Never Even Called Me By My Name." In the mid-80s, he had a number-one hit with "The Ride." To date, he has recorded 43 albums under his own name and estimates he has appeared on 74 in all.

Another dimension to David Allan Coe is movie acting. He played in *Stagecoach* and *The Last Days of Frank and Jesse James* with fellow outlaws Willie Nelson, Waylon Jennings, Johnny Cash and Kris Kristofferson. He has also appeared as himself in two movies on the life of Elvis Presley: *The Living Legend* and *Lady Grey*.

David and wife, Jody Lynn, currently reside in Branson, Missouri.

Take This Salsa And Eat It!

Great for any Mexican food or just with chips!

1 (8 oz) can tomato sauce
2 (8 oz) cans tomatoes and green chiles
2 (4 oz) cans chopped green chiles
1 (4 oz) can jalapeño relish
2 Tbsp salt

1 Tbsp black pepper
1 Tbsp crushed red pepper
3 bunches green onions, chopped
jalapeños, chopped: 3 for mild, 6 for
  medium, 9 for hot

For smoother texture run sauce through a food processor.

CONFEDERATE RAILROAD

Chattanooga native Danny Shirley, whose soulful vocals highlight the Confederate Railroad sound, has led the group since 1981. He is joined by drummer Mark DuFresne (a charter member of the group), guitarist Michael Lamb, keyboardist Chris McDaniel, bassist Wayne Secrest and pedal steel guitarist Gates Nichols. The group came up on the rocky side of country music, working as the road band for "outlaw" acts like David Allen Coe and Johnny Paycheck. They also did a long stint at "Miss Kitty's Club" in Kennesaw, Georgia, where they shared rotating house band duties (two weeks on, four weeks off) with such future stars as Travis Tritt, Billy Ray Cyrus, Little Texas and Diamond Rio.

The group's debut Atlantic album, *Confederate Railroad*, seemed to be what the country music world was waiting for. Their Top 10 single, "Trashy Women," became a dance club favorite and the raucous "Queen Of Memphis" was the number-one dance floor cut for six weeks. In May 1993, the album went gold and the group won the Academy of Country Music's Best New Vocal Group award. Their second album, *Notorious*, has already produced the hit single "Daddy Never Was The Cadillac Kind" and promises several more hits.

NOTORIOUS BARBEQUE SAUCE

6 cups brown sugar
⅓ cup paprika
6 Tbsp salt
6 Tbsp dry mustard
6 tsp chili powder

6 tsp cayenne pepper
1½ cups worchestershire sauce
3 cups ketchup
6 cups water
1 cup Crown Royal liquor

Mix all dry spices together, then add remaining ingredients. Simmer on low for 3 – 4 hours. Serve with chicken, beef or pork. You can marinate meat in vinegar for several hours before cooking with sauce. This recipe makes 2½ gallons of sauce.

MICKEY GILLEY

Mickey Gilley grew up close to his cousins Jerry Lee Lewis and Jimmy Lee Swaggart, learning to play the piano with them and sneaking near the windows of clubs to hear authentic rhythm and blues music while growing up in Ferriday, Louisiana. Mickey moved to Houston when he was seventeen, and shortly afterward his cousin Jerry Lee had his first hit. Mickey went to see him in concert in Houston and took him to the airport after the show. "He pulled out a big wad of hundred dollar bills," Mickey recalls, "and it made me decide right then that I was in the wrong business."

Mickey began performing in Houston nightclubs and recorded his first song in Memphis for Dot Records. Eventually, he took up residence at the Nesadel Club in Houston and quickly became one of the city's most popular acts. Then, in the early 70s, he opened Gilley's. The famous nightclub in Pasadena, Texas, was once billed as "The World's Largest Honky Tonk" and helped elevate country music to new heights when it served as the setting for *Urban Cowboy*, a landmark film in the annals of American culture.

During his career, Mickey has achieved a remarkable 39 Top 10 country hits, with seventeen of those songs reaching the number-one spot on the country charts. He is among a select few country singers who have achieved the honor of being recognized with a star on the Hollywood Walk of Fame.

GILLEY'S DEWBERRY OR BLACKBERRY JELLY

4 cups blackberries
5½ cups sugar

1 box Sure-Jell

Barely cover berries with water after they have been washed. Cook for 10 minutes. Let cool and strain out seeds. Flour sifter may be used to strain seeds. For 4 cups of berry juice, use 5½ cups of sugar and 1 box of Sure-Jell. Cook until bubbles up and then lower heat and cook for 5 minutes.

THE KENTUCKY HEADHUNTERS

The Kentucky HeadHunters are more "relative" than ever. Two of the five bandmembers, Fred Young, the drummer, and Richard Young, the rhythm guitarist, are brothers. Two others, lead guitarist Greg Martin and bass player Anthony Kenney are first cousins to the Youngs. Lead singer Mark Orr, may not be a blood relative, but he's "family" all the same—a close friend and musical blood brother of twenty-some years. Back in the early 80s, all five of these guys were members of a group called Itchy Brother (before that Itchy Brother was a widely popular Kentucky based band in the late 60s), which was "kind of a musical grand-dad" to the present-day Kentucky HeadHunters.

Along the way, the HeadHunters have picked up rave reviews and a bounty of awards. They've hauled home a Grammy award, two back-to-back Country Music Association Group of the Year citations, and similar laurels from the Academy of Country Music (Group of the Year, 1990) and *Playboy* magazine's Album of the Year.

"After 25 years together, off and on, you can tell this ain't just a band of five boys makin' music," says Richard Young. "It's teamwork, love, brotherhood and havin' a good time. After all, that's what music was created for, isn't it? I know ours was."

YOU'LL RAVE ON ABOUT HOT PEPPER RELISH

48 cayenne peppers
7 medium onions
2 Tbsp whole mustard seed

2 Tbsp salt
3 cups vinegar
3 cups white granulated sugar

Grind peppers and onions together and mix with other ingredients and boil at least 35 minutes. Put this in sealed sterilized jars.

HAL KETCHUM

Although he now resides in Nashville, Hal Ketchum was born (on April 9, 1953) and raised in Greenwich, New York. A drummer since high school, he also had a notebook full of song ideas but didn't give much thought to songwriting until he began attending Gruene Hall's Sunday afternoon singer/songwriter sessions, which boasted the likes of Townes Van Zandt, Jimmie Dale Gilmore, Guy Clark, Joe Ely, Robert Earl Keen, Jr. and Butch Hancock.

It was just about five years ago that he gave up his job as a carpenter and a cabinet maker to "go for it" in Nashville. "This is all relatively new to me," he says. "The past few years have been a whirlwind, so it's only been lately that I've been able to sit back and be comfortable with who I am in the middle of all this." In June 1992, his debut release, *Past The Point Of Rescue*, was certified gold. The album produced four Top 10 singles: "Smalltown Saturday Night," "I Know Where Love Lives," "Past The Point Of Rescue" and "Five O'clock World."

His second album is the acclaimed *Sure Love*.

Hal is married to Terrell Pye, the co-owner of Forerunner Music, the largest music publisher in Nashville. Although they live in Music City, his favorite place is still New York. His favorite band is Tom Petty and The Heartbreakers and his favorite country singer is George Jones. In his spare time, Hal loves to paint and write children's stories.

YOU'LL SURE LOVE MY
HOT ARTICHOKE SEAFOOD DIP

2 (14 oz) cans artichoke hearts, drained
    and chopped
2 cups mayonnaise
2 cups grated parmesan cheese

12 oz. crab meat or cooked shrimp and crab
    combination
½ cup seasoned bread crumbs

Combine artichokes, mayonnaise, cheese and seafood. Spoon into greased 1½-quart dish. Top with crumbs. Bake at 325° for 15 – 20 minutes. Serve with crackers.

DICKEY LEE

Dickey Lee released his first record in 1957. "Dream Boy" became a local hit in Memphis, but it was in 1961 that he received national recognition when his song "Patches" became a number-one pop hit and million-selling record. His follow-up release, "I Saw Linda Yesterday," also rocketed to the top of the charts.

In 1971, Dickey signed with RCA and recorded as one of that label's top country artists for ten years with such hits as "9,999,999 Tears" and "Never Ending Song of Love." A hit songwriter, as well as a hit artist, he penned such country favorites as "The Door is Always Open" (number one for Dave and Sugar), "I'll Be Leaving Alone" (number one for Charley Pride), "You're the First Time I've Thought About Leaving" (number one for Reba McEntire), "In a Different Light" (number one for Doug Stone) and the number-one hit for George Jones, "Let's Fall to Pieces Together." Dickey also wrote the country standard, "She Thinks I Still Care," which was a number-one hit for George Jones, Elvis and Anne Murray. The recipient of fifteen BMI awards, one Country Music Association Finalist Award and one Grammy nomination, Dickey's songs have also been hits for Kenny Rogers, Merle Haggard, Waylon Jennings, Marty Robbins, Brenda Lee, Tracy Byrd, James Taylor, Emmylou Harris, Kathy Mattea and a list that goes on for a mile.

When Dickey is not writing, he can be found on the road performing on the rock and roll revival shows. He lives in Nashville.

She Knows I Still Care For Corn Relish

1 (12 oz) can whole kernel corn
1 tsp mustard seed
½ tsp dry mustard
¼ tsp salt
¼ tsp pepper

⅓ cup cider vinegar
4 Tbsp light brown sugar
½ cup chopped onion
2 canned pimentos, chopped
¼ cup green peppers, chopped

Drain liquid from corn into saucepan, stir in mustard seed, mustard, salt, pepper, vinegar and brown sugar; bring to a boil. Combine corn, onion, pimento and green peppers in a bowl; pour hot liquid over corn mixture, stir lightly. Cover and refrigerate over night. Makes about 2 cups.

DAN SEALS

Dan Seals was raised in West, Texas. His father grew up with Ernest Tubb, and his brother Jim was the Texas State Champion Fiddler when he was nine years old. Jim would also go on to fame with Seals and Crofts, while Dan would achieve his first success as half of England Dan and John Ford Coley. Their record "I'd Really Love To See You Tonight," recorded in Hendersonville, Tennessee (just outside of Nashville), sold over two million copies. As a solo artist, Dan Seals has been topping the country charts consistently since 1985.

Despite the years of pop and country stardom he has achieved, Dan has maintained a healthy perspective about the business, focusing on the work rather than on the trappings. "Some people are more in love with being a star and driving around in the car than they are in actually doing the work of having great songs and great material," Dan reflects. "The idea of hungering after being a star is so empty, because it doesn't give anything back. It's hard to stay excited about riding in limousines, because when you get outside of any large city and they get you a limousine, it comes from the funeral parlor. It ain't there, you know? I'd rather just work and leave all that stuff out of it."

TEXAS CAVIAR
I'D REALLY LOVE TO HAVE SOME TONIGHT

½ lb black-eyed peas (1½ cups = ½ lb)
1 cup green pepper, diced
¼ cup pimentos, diced
1 cup onions, diced
½ cup green onions, finely chopped

2 Tbsp chopped garlic
¼ cup jalapeño peppers, seeded and finely
  chopped
1 cup bottled Italian dressing
salt and pepper

Soak peas in cold water to cover overnight. Drain and rinse. Cover with fresh water and bring to a boil. Reduce heat, cover and simmer 1 hour or longer until tender. Do not overcook. Drain, rinse and place peas in large bowl. Add green peppers, pimentos, onions, green onions, garlic, jalapeños and dressing. Add salt and pepper to taste. Makes 4 cups.

GEORGE STRAIT

George Strait was born on May 18, 1952 in Pearsall, Texas. A country music great since 1981, when he was selected *Billboard* magazine's New Male Album Artist of the Year and *Record World*'s New Male Artist of the Year, he has experienced a phenomenal career. Since his beginning, he has reached the number-one position on the country charts more often than any other solo performer.

He has been honored as Male Vocalist of the Year by the Academy of Country Music in 1984, 1985 and 1988 and by the Country Music Association in 1985 and 1986; and as Entertainer of the Year by the ACM in 1989 and by the CMA in 1989 and 1990. The American Music Awards

selected him Top Male Country Vocalist in 1991, and 1993 found him accepting the Academy of Country Music's Tex Ritter Award.

George Strait moved with characteristic ease into the role of film actor. In October 1992, the film *Pure Country* was released and became one of the most successful movies of the year. The movie soundtrack also saw George attain new heights. It became the biggest seller of his career and, at last count, was charging toward the three million mark in sales.

A member of the Professional Rodeo Cowboys Association, George enjoys steer-roping, fishing, skiing and golf. He and his wife Norma have one son, George, Jr., known as "Bubba."

STRAIT AHEAD STRAWBERRY JAM

4 cups prepared fruit
7 cups sugar

2 Tbsp lemon juice
½ bottle liquid pectin

To prepare fruit, use about 2 quarts small, fully ripe strawberries. Spread about half of berries in a single layer and press gently to a thickness of ¼" with bottom of tumbler. This crushes centers of berries without breaking skins.

Measure sugar and fruit into separate dishes. Put layer of pressed berries into large kettle and cover with layer of sugar. Continue to alternate layers of pressed berries and sugar until all have been used, having sugar on top. Add lemon juice. Let stand overnight or at least 5 hours. Mix well, and bring to a full rolling boil over hottest fire. Stir constantly before and while boiling. Boil hard 3 minutes. Remove from fire and stir in liquid pectin. Ladle off a few glasses of hot clear syrup for jelly. (To separate syrup from fruit, press a sieve into jam.) Then stir and skim jam by turns for just 5 minutes to cool slightly, in order to prevent floating fruit. Pour quickly. Paraffin hot jelly and jam at once. Makes 2 – 3 glasses jelly and 7 – 8 glasses jam (6 oz size).

SHEB WOOLEY

Sheb Wooley was born in Eric, Oklahoma, on April 10, 1921. As a teenager, he was a skilled rodeo rider, which later served him well in Hollywood. When he was fifteen, he had his own band, The Plainview Melody Boys, and in 1945, he took off for Nashville in hopes of making his mark. He recorded four sides at the WSM radio studio, some of the first records ever to be recorded in Nashville.

Sheb left for Hollywood with the idea of getting into films. In an amazingly short time, he landed a screen test at Warner Brothers and a part in his first film, *Rocky Mountain*, starring Errol Flynn. Over the years, he has appeared in over seventy films including *High Noon* with Gary Cooper and Grace Kelly, *War Wagon* with John Wayne and *Giant* with James Dean and Elizabeth Taylor. Most recently he appeared in *Starman* and *Hoosiers*.

In the late 50s came his long-running role on the TV series *Rawhide*, and his surprise novelty hit record, "Purple People Eater." "I got the idea when this friend of mine told me his son came home from school with a joke about a people eater," remembers Sheb. "I wrote the song, just dashed it off as sort of an afterthought." He recorded the song, but MGM didn't want to release it until the company's New York office heard it. "Young people up there would gather around and listen to it," says Sheb. "Pretty soon, every lunch time, there'd be 40 or 50 of 'em playing it. The front office saw what was going on, reconsidered and released the record. It took off and just went crazy."

WILD 'N WOOLEY SUPER-TURBO PICANTE

10 fresh jalapeño peppers
10 fresh habanero peppers
2 fresh red chile peppers
2 green peppers
10 red tomatoes
10 tomatillos
½ Tbsp cayenne pepper
¼ Tbsp white pepper
⅛ Tbsp black pepper

Utensils needed:
little knife
big bowl

10 ripe Vidalia onions–or any other
sweet onion
1 bunch parsley
3 bunches cilantro/coriander
Mexican oregano
juice of 1 lemon
20 green onions
3 cups distilled vinegar
1 cup sugar

gas mask
fire extinguisher

Puree the jalapeños, habaneros and red chile peppers. Add vinegar and sugar. Jump up and down three times fast while tossing in the cayenne, white and black peppers. Do a 3 minute raindance...then dice the red tomatoes, tomatillos and green peppers and Vidalia and green onions. Do five somersaults before chopping the parsley and cilantro. Throw into the big bowl along with lemon juice. Turn around three times and shout "Ole!!" Add coriander and Mexican oregano, along with any other spices you might like, so the picante won't be so bland. Mix all ingredients together and seal very tightly. Dig a hole in the yard by the light of the full moon. Cover bowl with dirt...let sit for 6 hours, 5 minutes and 47 seconds. Then douse yourself with holy water, dig up the bowl, grab a bag of taco chips and a gallon of sour cream. Say a quick prayer and dig in!!! (For fullest flavor, recipe must be made at the third hour of the full moon.... The fire extinguisher is optional.)

BREADS, ROLLS & BISCUITS

MARK CHESTNUTT

Born in Beaumont, Texas, on September 6, 1963, Mark Chestnutt has been living and breathing country music all his life. He started out singing along with his father's Hank Williams records, then did his best to imitate George Jones. Today he is a collector of old country records, and he looks to the "classics" for inspiration. "I still listen to things that were cut over 30 years ago," he says. "And I always hear something new."

Mark's father, the late Bob Chestnutt, had several singles on an independent Nashville label in the late 60s and early 70s, so as soon as Mark showed a serious interest in becoming a country singer, his father was behind him all the way. Mark quit school in the eleventh grade to play music full time. "My daddy told me if I was gonna quit school that I would have to be damn sure that I was gonna really work hard at music, because I wouldn't be able to do anything else—which was fine with me because I didn't want to do anything else."

By the time he was seventeen, Mark had made a total of eight records for independent labels in Texas. He began making trips to Nashville, and that led to his signing with MCA. Half of the songs on his debut album, *Too Cold At Home*, became hit singles and the album certified gold. His second album, *Longnecks and Short Stories*, yielded four more hits and also achieved gold record status.

OL' COUNTRY PUMPKIN BREAD

1 cup sugar
½ cup brown sugar, firmly packed
1 cup canned pumpkin
½ cup oil
2 eggs

2 cups flour
1 tsp baking soda
½ tsp each: salt, nutmeg and cinnamon
¼ tsp ginger
½ cup nuts, chopped

Combine sugars, pumpkin, oil and eggs in bowl; beat well. Sift dry ingredients together. Add pumpkin mixture, mixing well. Stir in nuts and ¼ cup water. Pour into well-greased 9" x 5" x 3" loaf pan. Bake at 350° for 1 hour and 15 minutes or until bread tests done.

ROY CLARK

Born on April 15, 1933, in Meherrin, Virginia, Roy Clark is one of the great entertainers of the world. The first instrument he ever played was a cigar box with a ukulele neck and four strings rigged up by his father. On his fourteenth Christmas, his parents gave him the real thing—a Silvertone model guitar from Sears.

Roy's achievements are numerous. He is celebrating his 24th anniversary as host of the ever popular TV show *Hee Haw*. This number-one syndicated show is carried by stations across the country and is viewed by 30 million fans weekly. Roy became the first National Ambassador for UNICEF, which was a great personal honor for him. Among his prestigious awards are Entertainer of the Year from the Academy of Country Music and the Country Music Association, Comedy Act of the Year by the Academy of Country Music, Country Music Star of the Year by the American Guild of Variety Artists, Picker of the Year in *Playboy's* Reader's Poll, Best Country Guitarist from *Guitar* magazine, and the list goes on.

Roy has been married to his wife Barbara Joyce since August 31, 1957. They currently live in Tulsa, Oklahoma, where, in his spare time, Roy enjoys driving and tinkering with his collection of wonderful classic cars from the 30s to the 60s. He has recently completed his autobiography, *Roy Clark...My Life, In Spite of Myself* with Marc Eliot for Simon & Schuster.

THE PICKER'S PICK OF APPLE MUFFINS

2 cups whole wheat flour
1 Tbsp liquid Sweet 'n' Low
1 Tbsp baking powder
1 pinch salt

1 egg
1 cup lowfat milk
¼ cup applesauce

Preheat oven to 400°. Spray 12 muffin cups with Pam or grease with Mazola. In large bowl with fork, mix flour, baking powder and salt. In small bowl with fork, beat egg slightly, then stir milk, applesauce and liquid sweetener into beaten egg. Add egg mixture to flour mixture and with spoon, stir just until flour is moistened. Spoon batter into sprayed or greased muffin-pan cups. Bake muffins 22 – 25 minutes until they are well risen and toothpick inserted in center of one comes out clean. Immediately remove muffins from pan onto wire rack; serve at once, or keep warm by leaving in cups tipped slightly so steam escapes. Now just enjoy these delicious, healthy muffins with loved ones!

MARK COLLIE

Halfway between the rockabilly blues of Memphis and the country traditions of Nashville, lies the heart, the music and the home of Mark Collie. Waynesboro, a small town near the Tennessee River, is where he cut his musical teeth. As one of six children, Mark enjoyed a captive audience playing piano and guitar, and as a child he developed a love of performing that remains evident in his live shows today. "My musical roots are like the roots of a tree," he says. "They go a long way in every direction."

Mark's first release, "Even the Man in the Moon Is Cryin' " reached number three on the national country charts. He co-wrote the song with Don Cook, one of Nashville's hottest producers. It was their first attempt at collaboration and their relationship evolved naturally into the kind of producer–artist partnership that Mark was looking for. He says, "I needed someone who would allow me to be myself. I'm only good at being me, you know." Prior to his first success as a singer, his songs were recorded by Aaron Tippin, Randy Travis, Martina McBride and Marty Stuart.

Mark recently completed a TV commercial campaign for Oldsmobile that ran in the Middle Tennessee area and is being considered for various regional use throughout the country. He has also completed a radio spot campaign for McDonald's to be aired nationally.

BORN TO LOVE A CINNAMON SWEET ROLL

1 slice soft white bread
1 Tbsp cream-style cottage cheese
½ tsp sugar

⅟₁₆ tsp cinnamon
⅛ tsp vanilla
10 seedless raisins

Roll bread with a rolling pin until flat. Mash together the cheese, sugar, cinnamon and vanilla. Spread cheese mixture on bread; scatter raisins across center only. Roll like a jelly roll and fasten with toothpicks. Broil 3 – 4" below broiler until lightly toasted.

BILLY RAY CYRUS

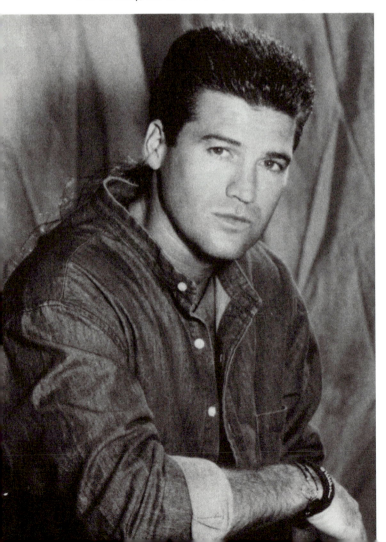

Billy Ray Cyrus was a somber kid. A quiet youngster deeply affected by his parent's divorce when he was five. Born August 25, 1961, he was raised in the small Kentucky town of Flatwoods. As a teenager, his place was on the athletic field and his hero was Johnny Bench.

At twenty, he followed an "intuition, an inner voice" that told him to buy a guitar. He formed a band called Sly Dog and soon they were a popular attraction in Ohio, Kentucky and West Virginia. In 1984 Billy Ray went to Los Angeles and spent two years trying for a recording contract. He ended up selling cars at an Oldsmobile dealership before heading back east. For four years he played five nights a week at the Ragtime Lounge in Huntington, West Virginia. On his two days off, he'd make the six-hour drive to Nashville to visit offices on Music Row with photos, nightclub credentials and his songs. He felt the sting of rejection but says, "I just stayed focused on my objectives. I just always believed."

After five years of perseverance, he signed a contract with Mercury Records in 1990. "Achy Breaky Heart" appeared as his debut video in March 1992. The accompanying dance step swept through the nation's country dance emporiums like prairie fire. His album, *Some Gave All*, sold more than nine million copies during the first twelve months of its release and earned Billy Ray honors from the World Music Awards, the People's Choice Awards, the Country Music Association and the Recording Industry Association of America.

ACHY BREAKY GARLIC BREAD STICKS

6 wiener buns
¼ cup garlic spread
¼ cup butter or margarine

¼ cup Parmesan cheese, grated
Poppy or sesame seeds

Cut wiener buns in half lengthwise, cut again lengthwise to make sticks. Melt garlic and butter together and spread on sticks. Sprinkle with grated cheese and poppy or sesame seeds. Place on cookie sheet and toast in hot oven at 450° for about 8 minutes. Serve hot. Makes 24 sticks. Excellent with green salads and Italian dishes.

JOE DIFFIE

Perhaps one of the most important lessons that Joe Diffie has learned is his hard work ethic. Long a workingman, with years and years of foundry experience supplemented by a term stacking guitars on the dock at the Gibson Guitar plant and a long stint in the oil fields, he knows that nothing comes easy. Joe was born on December 28th in Duncan, Oklahoma, and believed he would grow up to be a chiropractor!

Joe signed with Epic Records in 1990, and his debut single, "Home," went straight to number one. So did his next five releases: "If You Want Me To," "If the Devil Dances," "New Way to Light Up an Old Flame," "Is It Cold in Here" and "Ships That Don't Come In" (the song he says he "wishes he had written"). He has been nominated for two Academy of Country Music awards, two TNN/*Music City News*

awards, a Country Music Association award and a Grammy.

When he's not touring with his band, Heartbreak Highway, he makes his home in Nashville and likes to work out and play golf. He is also a race car enthusiast. Joe claims his favorite song of all time is "He Stopped Loving Her Today" by George Jones.

DAD AND GRAN'S BREAD
(FROM JOE'S FATHER, JOE, AND GRANDMOTHER, LAVERNA)

1 Tbsp sugar
9 cups hot tap water
1 cup honey
¾ cup oil
3 Tbsp salt or light salt

2 cups raw bran (wheat)
1 cup raw wheat germ
5 lbs whole wheat flour
2 lbs white flour
6 pkgs dry yeast

In separate bowl mix ½ – ¾ cup of warm water with yeast and 1 Tbsp sugar. Stir. Set aside to activate a few minutes… meanwhile… mix 9 cups of hot tap water in huge bowl with honey, oil and salt. Stir in activated yeast mixture. Then stir in wheat flour combined with bran and wheat germ until dry enough to knead on counter top. Knead in white flour until dough is only slightly sticky to touch. Separate into 6 greased bread pans and let rise on warm stove top until bread rises about ⅓ or ¾ size of a loaf. Bake 20 minutes in preheated oven at 400°. Then bake 45 minutes at 300°. (Remember to lower your oven temperature for the last 45 minutes of baking!!!) Total baking time: 1 hour, 45 minutes. Remove from oven, baste all sides lightly with margarine. Let loaves cool sitting crossways on top of bread pans. Wrap bread in tin foil, freeze and/or eat when ready!

THE GATLIN BROTHERS

Larry, Steve and Rudy are the Gatlin Brothers. "Larry was the oldest, and he knew the songs and was big enough to carry the lead," remembers Rudy. "Steve and I just seemed to always know how to harmonize. Mom and Dad would help us refine our parts in those early years, but just like you don't remember walking for the first time, we seemed to be able to harmonize together from the very start." At the boys' first public performance, Larry, Steve and Rudy were only seven, four and two-and-a-half, respectively, but they won first prize at an Abilene talent show.

By the early 70s, while the brothers were still in college, Larry moved to Nashville where he began establishing himself as a songwriter. He also sang harmony on some of Kris Kristofferson's early records and began having his songs cut by Kris, Johnny Cash and Dottie West. By the mid-70s, Steve and Rudy and their sister LaDonna were opening and singing backup for Tammy Wynette. Once "Broken Lady" hit (and earned them their first Grammy), the decision to team full-time with Larry and "go for it" seemed the only logical one, and the rest is history.

Today there's a 2,000-seat Gatlin Brothers Theatre, a state-of-the-art concert venue within the Waccamaw Harbour entertainment complex, that will headline Gatlin performances approximately six months a year. In August 1992, they saw the opening of the Gatlin Brothers Music City Grille in the Mall of America in Bloomington, Minnesota. A second Grille opened in Sacramento in November 1993. These Texas-style eateries and 750-seat nightclubs are so successful that discussions are underway concerning franchises in other cities.

MEXICAN CORNBREAD IS WORTH ALL THE GOLD IN CALIFORNIA

1 Tbsp cooking oil
2 cups yellow cornmeal
1 cup flour
2 tsp baking powder
1 tsp salt

1 Tbsp sugar
2 jalapeño peppers, seeded and chopped
1 cup grated cheddar cheese
2 eggs
1 (8 oz) can cream style corn

Preheat oven to 425°. In a 9" x 13" baking dish, preheat 1 Tbsp cooking oil while mixing the cornbread. Mix the first five dry ingredients together. Mix peppers, cheese, corn and eggs, stirring well. Combine with the dry ingredients. Pour batter into the hot baking dish. Bake 1 hour, or until brown on top and a knife inserted in the center comes out clean.

WAYLON JENNINGS

It was Waylon Jennings who gave up his seat to the Big Bopper on the plane that crashed, killing the Big Bopper, Buddy Holly and Ritchie Valens. Waylon met Buddy Holly in 1955 in Littlefield, Texas, on local station KLLL's *Sunday Dance Party*, where Waylon and his band made regular guest appearances. It was Buddy Holly who produced Waylon's first record, and he became Buddy's protege until the tragic plane crash. "Mainly what I learned from Buddy," Waylon says, "was an attitude. He loved music, and he taught me that it shouldn't have any barriers to it."

In the early to mid-60s, Waylon was headlining a club called JD's in Phoenix. Word got out about his rough-edged, soulful vocal style that borrowed from rock and rockabilly. That led to a short stint at A & M Records before Chet Atkins signed him to RCA. In November 1993, RCA announced his historic re-signing to the label.

In 1976, Waylon helped found a movement that would change the face of country. He and Willie Nelson, Tompall Glaser and Jessi Colter (who has been married to Waylon since 1969) teamed up for *Wanted: The Outlaws*. It became the first platinum album ever recorded in Nashville and helped Waylon and Willie sweep that year's Country Music Association Awards, winning Best Album, Best Single and Best Vocal Duo.

OVEN-ICE BOX ROLLS ARE SO GOOD THEY SHOULD BE OUTLAWED

From the kitchen of JESSI COLTER.

1½ cups milk
¾ cup sugar
1½ tsp salt
1 cup oil

2 eggs
6 cups flour
2 pkgs dry yeast

Heat milk until hot or until skim forms. Add sugar, salt, oil and eggs to a mixing bowl and mix well; add milk. Slowly add 3 cups of flour. Put yeast in ½ cup warm water. Let this stand for 5 minutes and then add to the above mixture. Cover and place in the oven for 1 hour on warm. Remove from oven and stir in 3 more cups of flour. Place in the refrigerator for as little as 1 hour or as long as 2 days. I always do this a day ahead. Several hours before you plan to serve them, roll them out on a floured board. Cut in small circles. Dip in melted butter and fold in half. Secure the roll by pressing with your finger lightly in the middle. Place on a cookie sheet and cover very lightly. Let them rise for at least 4 hours. I usually make them early in the moring and let them rise until evening. Bake at 400° for about 15 minutes or until lightly browned. This roll will bring joy to all who love hot breads. It is Waylon's very favorite. Be sure to make plenty, as each guest will eat several.

51

RONNIE MILSAP

The story of Ronnie Milsap's ascent to stardom is a legendary one in music history. A native of the Great Smoky Mountains of North Carolina, he was born with congenital cataracts. Blind, but with another kind of vision, he attended North Carolina's State School for the Blind where he started playing music ranging from classical to rock and roll. Although he started college as a pre-law major, he soon realized his heart was in his music.

He started his recording career on New York's Scepter label in the mid-60s, scoring several R & B hits before coming to the attention of Elvis Presley. Elvis hired the young singer/keyboardist to play on several of his recordings, including "Kentucky Rain." In 1973, Ronnie signed to RCA Records and put his unmistakable touch on country music. The following year he won his first Grammy for Best Country Performance, Male for "Please Don't Tell Me How the Story Ends." He continued to win Grammys in 1976, 1981, 1983 and 1985. He was the Country Music Association's Entertainer of the Year in 1974 and 1977. Ronnie has won virtually every award a performer could hope for including the Academy of Country Music's Best Male Vocalist in 1983 and ACM's Song of the Year Award in 1986. In 1982, his multi-format hit "Any Day Now" became *Billboard's* Song of the Year.

Today, Ronnie records for Liberty Records and stands as one of country music's true superstars.

ANY DAY NOW I'LL MAKE SMALL CHEESE BISCUITS

½ cup sharp cheddar cheese
½ cup butter
½ tsp salt
⅛ tsp red pepper

1 – 1½ cups all- purpose flour
paprika

Grate cheese and let set outside refrigerator overnight, covered. Work cheese and soft butter with hands until pliable. Add flour and seasoning and work until soft. Pinch off small balls, and on a cookie sheet flatten out to about the size of a quater, very thin. Bake at 325° for 15 minutes, and when done, sprinkle with paprika.

These biscuits will keep in refrigerator or in tins for as long as 2 – 3 weeks.

TOMMY OVERSTREET

Tommy Overstreet had his first major hit record in 1971. His recording of "Gwen Congratulations" reached the number-one spot in the United States, Canada and Australia. Over the next ten years, he had 26 consecutive Top 10 hits, including four gold records. He has made more European tours than just about any other artist (30 to date) and was voted as the "number two favorite" in Europe—preceded only by Johnny Cash.

Born in Houston, Texas, Tommy began his career at the age of thirteen when he started performing with his late "Uncle" Gene Austin (the first major recording star of the 20s and 30s known for his hit "My Blue Heaven") throughout the United States. He toured with Gene for six years and then relocated to Nashville in the late 60s to develop his own style in country music and sign with Dot Records.

In June 1985, Tommy was the first recognized music personality to move to Branson, Missouri. It had been described to him as "a cross between Las Vegas and Mayberry," but Tommy praised the area as a homeplace with the opportunity to perform and work at home. He'd been traveling on the road for so many years he was anxious to break

new ground in an area he felt held all the qualities of the creative atmosphere he loves so much. He does, however, continue to travel, perform on television and produce and write songs. He is presently working on two new albums.

T.O.'s Crescent Rolls

5 cups all-purpose flour, divided, 1 cup &
  4 cups
¼ cups sugar
2 pkgs dry yeast
2 tsp salt

1 cup water
¾ cup milk
¼ cup vegetable oil
1 egg
1½ sticks butter, softened

Combine 1 cup flour, sugar, yeast and salt in a large bowl. Combine water, milk and oil in saucepan and heat to very warm (120°). Blend into flour mixture, using electric mixer. Add egg and mix for 5 minutes. Cut butter into remaining flour with fingertips or use pastry cutter (flour will resemble coarse corn meal). Combine the two flour mixtures; blend well. Place dough in greased bowl turning once to grease top. Cover; chill 2 hours. Punch dough down; turn out onto floured board. Knead 4 – 5 times. Divide dough into 4 equal balls. Roll each ball out on floured board to form a ¼" thick circle. Cut into wedges. Roll each wedge up beginning with the wide end to form a tight roll. Place rolls on a greased baking sheet with the point against the pan. Cover and let rise in a warm place until doubled in bulk (about 30 minutes). Preheat oven to 400°. Bake for approximately 20 minutes or until golden brown. Makes 3 dozen rolls...and MAN ARE THEY GREAT!

TANYA TUCKER

Tanya Tucker has been winning over audiences from the time she was a child. She began her climb to stardom at the age of nine when her father (and her manager) Beau Tucker took her to Las Vegas to make a demo. By the time she was thirteen, she had one of the biggest hits in country music history, "Delta Dawn." By the time she was fifteen, she had a Grammy nomination, a "greatest hits" package and was one of the few country artists to ever grace the cover of *Rolling Stone* magazine.

In 1986, Tanya signed with Liberty Records (then Capitol) and started recording a new string of hit records. Together Tanya and her producer Jerry Crutchfield have created a pile of award nominations (Country Music Association, Academy of Country Music and Grammy awards) and over 25 hit singles. Her video for the number-one single, "Two Sparrows In A Hurricane" (from her platinum-selling Liberty album), won the Academy of Country Music's Video of the Year award.

To top off her incredible career, she's set to release an exercise video, "The Tanya Tucker Country Workout." It will be a low-impact workout program featuring dance and exercise routines.

There Won't Be Enough Sweet Southern Dressing Left For Two Sparrows

1 recipe cornbread (see below)
¾ cup butter
1 medium onion, diced
¼ cup chopped parsley
1¼ cup celery, diced
¾ tsp salt

½ tsp paprika
⅛ tsp nutmeg
2 large eggs, beaten
1½ cup pecans, chopped
mushrooms, diced
2 Tbsp white wine

Sauté onions in butter until soft. Add parsley, celery, salt, paprika, nutmeg, mushrooms and wine. Let simmer 2 – 3 minutes. Crumble prepared cornbread in food processor. Transfer cornbread to a large mixing bowl and add sautéed mixture, eggs and pecans. Mix well. Put in a well-buttered baking dish, cover and bake for 30 minutes at 350°.

Cornbread

1½ cup corn meal
⅓ cup whole wheat flour
1 tsp salt
1 tsp baking soda

1 egg, beaten
2 cups buttermilk
2 Tbsp honey

Mix dry ingredients together. Stir together egg, buttermilk and honey. Stir dry ingredients into wet ingredients until well mixed but not smooth. Bake in cast iron skillet at 350° for 20 minutes.

LEROY VAN DYKE

Leroy Van Dyke grew up on a 3,000 acre farm/ranch operation in central Missouri, and is fully conversant with cattle, hog, sheep, horse and mule production as well as hay and grain crops. He attended the University of Missouri-Columbia with a dual major: agricultural journalism and animal husbandry. He received a B.S. in agriculture and did one semester of graduate work. After serving in Korea as a special agent for the U.S. Army Counter-Intelligence Corps, he returned to civilian life as a fieldman in the purebred livestock advertising department at the *Chicago Drovers Journal*. While he was working at *Drovers*, he wrote and recorded the multi-million-selling record "Auctioneer" and was suddenly catapulted into show business.

Leroy followed his incredible first hit with another multi-million seller called "Walk On By," a record that stayed on the charts for 42 weeks and went to number one in every country in the free world. During his career he has recorded over 500 songs and released a total of 36 albums. He had the starring role in the movie *What Am I Bid?*, was a regular member of Red Foley's ABC-TV show, *Ozark Jubilee*, and hosted his own syndicated TV series, *The Leroy Van Dyke Show*. For ten years he co-hosted the most widely syndicated show in radio history, *Country Crossroads*, and was the first entertainer to receive the Country Music Association's Founding President's award. He was also the only country performer ever to open a show for Marilyn Monroe!

As Leroy moves into his 37th year in show business, he continues to travel in excess of one hundred thousand performance miles every year.

AUCTIONEER, WHAT AM I BID FOR MY DENVER BISCUITS?

From the kitchen of Irene Sims Van Dyke, mother of Leroy Van Dyke

1 pkg yeast
¼ cup warm water
4 cups milk, scalded
1 cup shortening
½ cup sugar

1 cup mashed potatoes
2 tsp salt
1 level tsp baking soda
2 heaping tsp baking powder
all-purpose flour

Soften active dry yeast in ¼ cup warm water. To scalded milk, add shortening and sugar. To milk mixture, add yeast mixture, mashed potatoes, salt, baking soda and baking powder. Then add enough sifted flour to make a soft dough. (For whole wheat biscuits or rolls, I use half all-purpose flour and half whole wheat flour.) Place in large, lightly greased bowl, cover and store in refrigerator; use dough as needed. Punch down if it rises too much. Dough will keep for several days in the refrigerator. When you are ready to make the biscuits, pull off the amount of dough you need, put on lightly floured surface, knead gently for a few seconds. Roll dough to ½" thick; cut with biscuit cutter. Place on greased cookie sheet, cover and let rest 10 minutes or longer. Bake in hot oven (400°) 10 – 12 minutes. This dough also makes excellent cinnamon rolls!

TRISHA YEARWOOD

Trisha Yearwood is the subject of a recent book, *Get Hot Or Go Home.* "It's not an authorized biography," explains Trisha, "but it is an authorized book. Basically it's a year in the life of country music. The author wanted to follow around an artist who was on the rise for one year. I don't know another artist who would do that, and I honestly don't know if I would do it again. But the result is a book that really shows the things that most people don't realize go on. We didn't censor anything. It's an honest book."

Trisha grew up on a farm in the small north Georgia town of Monticello. When she was five or six years old, a neighbor gave her a box of old Elvis records and she absorbed them. From Elvis she went on to absorb all the country artists in her parents' collection, southern rock and high school musicals. She arrived in Nashville midway through college in 1985. "Nashville," she admits, "took some adjustment." She finished her music business degree at Belmont College and got her foot in the door on Music Row as an intern in the publicity department of MTM Records. Gradually she began singing demos and then background vocals on master sessions. Before long, she was signed to MCA. Her first album yielded four hits. Her second album, *Hearts In Armor,* featured an all-star cast of harmony singers including Garth Brooks, Vince Gill, Emmylou Harris, Don Henley and Raul Malo (lead singer of The Mavericks). Her first two albums were certified platinum and she is featured in a nationwide TV ad campaign for Revlon cosmetics.

THE BOY LOVES MY SAVORY BUTTERMILK DRESSING

1 lb cornbread (from the recipe below or your own favorite)
½ lb toasted bread crumbs (make your own from ½ loaf of white bread cut into ½" cubes and toasted in slow oven until lightly browned)
¼ lb saltine crackers
½ medium onion, chopped fine
3 eggs, boiled and chopped
1 quart broth saved from baking turkey or hen, skim fat
salt & pepper to taste

Sauté onions in 2 Tbsp of fat till clear. Don't brown. In very large container (gallon or larger) crumble breads; add onion and eggs. Toss and add broth till mixture is well-moistened. (Clean hands make great mixers!) Add salt and pepper to taste. Turn into 9" x 13" baking pan which has been sprayed with non-stick cooking spray. Bake 15 minutes at 450° until lightly browned.

BUTTERMILK CORNBREAD

3 cups self-rising buttermilk cornbread mix
2 Tbsp melted butter or bacon drippings
2 – 3 cups buttermilk (enough to make a thick batter)

Mix all ingredients. Pour into well-greased 10" iron skillet. Bake at 450° till well browned—about 15 minutes. (Browned crust adds flavor if you are making dressing.)

CHILIS, SOUPS
& STEWS

THE BELLAMY BROTHERS

Born and bred in Darby, Florida, the Bellamy Brothers (Howard and David) grew up on land that's been a part of the Bellamy family for six generations. Their active cattle ranch now covers 2,500 acres. "We were raised about as country as you can get in Florida," says David. To give something back to the community where they were raised, the Bellamys host an annual benefit concert, The Snake Rattle and Roll Jam. Held in conjunction with

the Rattlesnake Festival each year in San Antonio, Florida, the "Jam" has benefited local, regional and national organizations since its 1989 premiere.

Their willingness to take chances led to their crossing over from the country to the pop charts long before it was fashionable. It resulted in their developing an immense following across Europe, where they've been major stars since the mid-70s. More recently, this spirit of accepting new challenges and blazing new ground led country music's longest-running successful duo to begin yet another bold venture—Bellamy Brothers Records. *Rip Off the Knob* (Howard and David's third album since forming the label) is receiving the same enthusiastic response as the previous two albums, *Best of the Best* and *The Latest and the Greatest.* "Every artist dreams of having total control over their own creativity," says Howard. "For us, the record company ended up being a sort of natural evolution of things. It had been something we'd always talked about in one way or another. It finally came to where the timing just seemed right."

Santa Fe Chili With a Cowboy Beat

Pinto beans
ground sirloin beef
fresh green chiles

garlic, chopped
onion, chopped
salt

Cook pinto beans in a crock pot until done. Fry ground beef in a frying pan, add garlic and onion to the beef; then cook beef to taste. Put whole fresh chiles into blender on medium, chop them until they're stringy. Add chili and ground beef to pinto beans, then add salt to taste.

65

GLEN CAMPBELL

An entertainment giant, Glen Campbell is a native of Delight, Arkansas, who started out early in music. When he was four, his father bought him a five-dollar Sears Roebuck guitar and within two years he was an accomplished picker. He left home at fourteen to pursue music full-time, and before long he was touring the Southwest with his own band.

At 24, Glen moved to Los Angeles where he immediately found work as a session guitarist, playing for such artists as Frank Sinatra, Nat King Cole, Merle Haggard and Elvis Presley. In the early 60s he signed with Capitol Records where he would have an incredibly successful recording career with hits such as "Gentle on My Mind," "By the Time I Get to Phoenix," "Galveston," "Wichita Lineman," "I Wanna Live," "The Dreams of the Everyday Housewife," "Rhinestone Cowboy" and "Southern Nights."

Glen has been named Male Vocalist of the Year by both the Country Music Association and the Academy of Country Music. CMA has also named him Entertainer of the Year. He has won Grammys, starred in his own TV series, *The Glen Campbell Goodtime Hour*, and co-starred with John Wayne in the film *True Grit*.

For the past three years, Glen has been a featured performer in Branson, Missouri, and opened the Glen Campbell Goodtime Theatre there on June 7, 1994. His autobiography, *Rhinestone Cowboy*, was released this year, and Glen undertook a national tour with its release.

GLEN'S FAVORITE CHILI ON A SOUTHERN NIGHT

½ lb dry pinto beans
5 cups canned peeled tomatoes
1 lb green bell peppers, seeded and coarsely chopped
1½ lbs onions, peeled and coarsely chopped
2 cloves garlic, crushed
1½ Tbsp olive oil

½ cup parsley, minced
2½ lbs hamburger meat (medium priced cut)
1 lb ground lean pork
⅓ cup chili powder
2 Tbsp salt
1½ tsp pepper
1½ tsp cumin seed

Soak pinto beans overnight in cold water in a large chili pot. Cover beans with fresh cold water and simmer for 2 hours. Note: Pouring out the water and rinsing the beans reduces gas effects. Sauté green bell peppers, onions, garlic and parsley in olive oil, add pork and hamburger. Brown and add spices and cook for 10 minutes. Combine all the above with beans and cook covered for one hour. Uncover and cook for another 30 minutes (add water if needed). This recipe makes 4 quarts.

RODNEY CROWELL

Rodney Crowell started out in the music business as an eleven-year-old drummer in his father's Western swing band in Houston. He soon realized that he wanted to be in the spotlight, and to do that he would have to play guitar. While he was learning, he began writing songs.

Rodney arrived in Nashville in 1972, and within two years was in Emmylou Harris's band. She recorded nine of his songs. Then Crystal Gayle put his music on the country charts with the hit single, "Till I Gain Control Again," and the Oak Ridge Boys scored with his "Leavin' Louisiana In The Broad Daylight."

In 1978, Rodney recorded his first solo album, *Ain't Living Long Like This*. The title song would become a country hit for Waylon Jennings. "Voila, An American Dream" became a pop hit for the Dirt Band, and Bob Seger had a hit with "Shame On The Moon." Rodney recorded three more albums, built a strong following on the road, and a strong reputation as the producer of hits for his then wife, Rosanne Cash. Finally, in 1988, he achieved the solo success he had wanted with *Diamonds And Dirt*. The album yielded five hit singles, including the Grammy winning "After All This Time."

The next few years were not easy. He and Rosanne divorced after twelve years of marriage, his father passed away and retirement looked very attractive. His friend Guy Clark provided the catalyst to get him going again when he stopped by and they wrote a song. Rodney's new album, *Let The Picture Paint Itself*, presents a fresh, new Rodney Crowell. "I'm not the same person I was two years ago," he says. "I closed some doors in my life so I could open new ones."

AFTER ALL THIS TIME
I'VE LEARNED TO MAKE LEEK SOUP

3 large leeks
1 medium onion
3 garlic cloves
2 cans chicken broth

1 (8 oz) can V-8 juice
1 cup water
1 sprig cilantro

Split leeks in half lengthwise, slice thin and wash thoroughly. Chop onions and garlic. Add leeks, onions and garlic to broth, V-8 and water and bring to a boil. Simmer for 45 minutes. Add cilantro.

CHARLIE DANIELS

Charlie Daniels grew up in North Carolina listening to country, bluegrass and rock and roll music. He started playing guitar in his early teens, then picked up mandolin and fiddle while playing in a bluegrass band throughout high school. After graduation, he worked days in a local plant and spent nights playing music with a Jacksonville band.

Deciding to pursue music full-time, he headed north and landed in Washington, D.C., where he formed a band called the Rockets and hit the road playing clubs. Changing their name to the Jaguars, they soon became one of the most popular bands throughout Texas, Oklahoma and Kansas.

In 1964, Elvis recorded one of Charlie's compositions, and in 1967, producer Bob Johnston convinced him to try his hand at session work in Nashville. He was invited to play on Bob Dylan's historic *Nashville Skyline* album and soon had an impressive list of credits as a Music City musician.

The Charlie Daniels Band became recording artists in 1970, and hit followed hit. In 1979, Charlie won a Grammy for Best Vocal Performance for "The Devil Went Down to Georgia." At the Country Music Association Awards that same year, he and the band not only picked up Single of the Year honors, but were named Band of the Year. Success continued, and in 1980 "In America" was nominated for the CMA's Song and Single of the Year.

In 1992, Charlie signed with Liberty Records to work with Jimmy Bowen. Look for musical possibilities to be redefined again.

THE DEVIL GOES DOWN TO GEORGIA FOR CHARLIE'S DIET CHILI

1 lb lean ground beef
1 medium onion, chopped
2 cups celery, diced
½ cup green pepper, chopped
½ tsp garlic salt

1 (15 oz) can red kidney beans, undrained
1 (2 lb) can tomatoes, undrained
1½ tsp chili powder
1 bay leaf

Brown ground beef and onions in dutch oven. Thoroughly drain. Add remaining ingredients. Simmer covered 1 – 2 hours.

Remove bay leaf. Serve hot. Freezes well. Makes 8 servings. 1 cup = 156 calories.

TOM T. HALL

In 1964, Tom T. Hall made the big move to Nashville, where he wrote songs eight hours a day, five days a week. In 1968, he recorded his first single for Mercury Records, but it was his song recorded by Jeannie C. Riley that same year that put him on the map. "Harper Valley PTA" was an international smash country-pop hit, selling over six million copies and winning Tom the Grammy for Song of the Year and the Country Music Association's Single of the Year.

Over the years, Tom has recorded 33 albums, has won 46 BMI Awards, been nominated for seven Country Music Association Awards and, for three consecutive years, was the National Truckers' Association Songwriter of the Year. He has written six books, including an autobiography, two songwriting textbooks, a collection of short stories and two novels. He has endorsed and been a spokesperson for Chevy Trucks, Tyson Chicken and Justin Boots. He has also acted as spokesperson for the Grand Ole Opry, of which he is a longtime member, and for the "Smokey the Bear" campaign for forest protection and conservation.

Today he manages a farm and works tirelessly for Animaland, a community animal shelter in Franklin, Tennessee. His business ventures have included owning a radio station, hosting his own TV show, operating a recording studio and serving as a board member of the Country Music Association. He is also a member of the Songwriters Hall of Fame. In recognition of his twenty years with Mercury/Polygram, the company has recently released *The Essential Tom T. Hall*, a collection of his favorite story songs.

OLD DOGS, CHILDREN, WATERMELON WINE AND SKINNY CHILI

2 lbs ground beef
2 (6 oz) cans tomatoes
1 (6 oz) can tomato paste
1 (6 oz) can pimentos
3 (6 oz) cans red kidney beans

chili powder, to taste
salt and pepper, to taste
3 medium onions, chopped
3 stalks celery, chopped
3 green bell peppers, chopped

Brown ground beef in skillet, stirring until crumbly; drain. Combine tomatoes, tomato paste, pimentos, beans and ground beef in stockpot; mix well. Simmer for 2 – 3 hours. Add chili powder, salt and pepper; mix well. Add onions, celery and green peppers. Cook for 20 minutes longer or just until vegetables are tender-crisp for a crunchy texture. Serve with corn bread or crackers. Serves 8.

TRACY LAWRENCE

In 1991, Tracy Lawrence was a wildly talented, up-and-coming young singer in Nashville who got his first headlines for a freakish incident. He suffered four gunshot wounds in a robbery attempt outside a motel in Nashville. His first album, which he'd just finished, was put on hold while he recovered from his wounds. Late that year *Sticks and Stones* came out, and nothing could stop either the album or Tracy Lawrence.

Tracy began performing when he was a teenager in Foreman, Arkansas. After attending Southern Arkansas University, he moved to Louisiana to join a band as a lead singer. When the group's routine of weekend gigs all over the South seemed to be leading nowhere, he packed up and headed for Nashville in the fall of 1990. In less than a year he had a recording contract with Atlantic Records.

With the success of *Sticks and Stones*, he found himself on the road again. Only this time it was different. "Being on the road helped take me to another level, as far as the demands you set for yourself.

When you work with so many great acts, you stop trying to play like a bar band. You start trying to be an entertainer, and you try to motivate yourself to do the best show you can—which isn't very hard to do when you're playing with people like George Jones."

STICKS AND STONES AND ARKANSAS STEW

1 lb beef, cubed
4 stalks celery, chopped
1 large onion, chopped
6 carrots, chopped
3 tsp salt

3 tsp black pepper
1 regular can green peas
¼ cup flour
2 quarts water
1 can beef stock

Brown beef in a skillet; remove beef and add flour slowly to grease from meat. Brown the flour and add approximately ½ cup of water, stirring constantly to prevent lumps. Pour flour mixture into a large pot. Add browned beef, onion, celery, salt, pepper, water and beef broth. Simmer for 30 minutes. Add more water or broth if thickens too much.

75

TIM MCGRAW

"I grew up listening to music," says Tim McGraw. "I sang along with the radio on everything from Motown to Merle Haggard. I always wanted to be a singer. But big dreams in small towns aren't given much respect. And in Start, Louisiana, being a singer didn't top the list of hot occupations." So Tim, like the rest of his friends, focused on sports and had aspirations of becoming a lawyer. After high school, he was offered several sports scholarships, but chose to attend Northeast Louisiana University because it was close to home and less expensive. That decision ultimately led to his career in music. "It was a big commuter school," remembers Tim, "and in the summer everybody left town. I got bored, bought a guitar and taught myself to play." By fall, with enough chords and tunes under his belt, he was playing the club circuit in northeastern Louisiana and Jacksonville, Florida.

Tim didn't grow up with his famous father, baseball pitcher Tug McGraw, but was raised by his mother and stepfather. "I never knew my dad until I was eighteen," he says. "There's a preconceived notion that I grew up this rich kid, the son of a baseball player. It wasn't like that at all."

Tim's second Curb album is titled *Not A Moment Too Soon*. The first single from the album, "Indian Outlaw," skyrocketed to number one and has broken request records all over the country. His self-titled debut album produced the hit single "Welcome To The Club," which led *Country America* magazine to accurately predict him as one of Country's Most Likely To Succeed in 1993.

OUTLAW McGRAW'S CAJUN GUMBO

1 chicken, cut into pieces
1 lb smoked hot sausage
4 Tbsp flour
3 cups okra (frozen is okay)
3 onions, chopped

1 bell pepper, chopped
3 stalks celery, chopped
3 cloves garlic, chopped
1 large can tomato sauce (optional)
2 Tbsp Tabasco sauce

Cut sausage into pieces and brown in a large pot. Remove sausage from grease. Add chicken and spices and brown thoroughly in sausage drippings. Remove chicken. Sprinkle flour in remaining oil, stirring constantly and cooking until it is a deep dark brown (roux). Add onions, pepper, celery and garlic and continue to stir until all thoroughly wilted. Return chicken and sausage to pot, add hot water, Tabasco sauce and tomato sauce if desired and let cook slowly until chicken is tender, 2 hours or longer. Serve over rice. Put on your favorite Tim McGraw CD. Enjoy!!

JODY MILLER

Grammy award winner Jody Miller was born in Blanchard, Oklahoma, the youngest of five sisters. She began singing in coffee houses after high school, and while performing in neighboring Norman, Oklahoma, she was seen by The Limeliters.

They suggested she contact their agent in Los Angeles, and soon Jody and her husband, Monty Brooks, had packed their bags and were heading west. One of her first stops was to see a fellow Oklahoman, actor Dale Robertson. She sang for him and he was so impressed that he called a friend at Capitol Records and she soon had her first recording contract. Within six months of signing with Capitol, she had her first hit, "He Walks Like A Man."

In the mid-60s, Jody was invited to perform the song "You Don't Have to Say You Love Me" at the San Remo Festival. The song had been written especially for her by Pino Dinnagio and Jody was the first person ever to record it. Upon returning to the States, she recorded her Grammy-winning hit "Queen of the House." In the 70s, she made the move to Epic Records and producer Billy Sherrill. She had an amazing string of successes with 24 chart records, eight chart albums, three Grammy award nominations and a Country Music Association nomination.

THE QUEEN OF THE HOUSE'S CAJUN STEW

2 pkgs cajun sausages, chopped bite-size
2 green peppers, chopped
1 quart pinto bean juice from the beans you had the day before (it's good to use your blender to puree the beans with the juice)

3 bunches green onion, chopped, using all the green
Louisiana Hot Sauce to taste (2 Tbsp)
worchestershire sauce to taste (2 – 3 Tbsp)
salt to taste (optional)

Sauté sausages in dutch oven (I use a heavy black iron pot). Transfer with slotted spoon to the lid of the pot. Sauté green onion and peppers until golden over medium-hot flame. Return sausages to pot, pouring bean juice over all. Season with salt, hot sauce and worchestershire. Bring to a boil and simmer 30 minutes. Serve with rice (or you can cook rice in the same pot as you simmer the dish).

THE NITTY GRITTY DIRT BAND

Today, The Nitty Gritty Dirt Band is composed of four band members: Jeff Hanna (vocals and guitar), Jimmie Fadden (vocals, drums and harmonica), Jimmy Ibbotson (vocals, bass, mandolin and guitar) and Bob Carpenter (vocals, keyboards and accordion). Jeff Hanna and Jimmie Fadden have been with the group since its inception in May 1966. Jimmy Ibbotson joined the group in 1969 and Bob Carpenter became a member in 1978. Former members of the group have included: Les Thompson, Bruce Kunkel, Ralph Barr, Jackson Browne, John McEuen, Chris Darrow, John Cable, Jackie Clark, Michael Buono, Al Garth, Richard Hathaway, Merle Brigante, Vic Mastriani, Michael Gardner and Bernie Leadon.

Their current Liberty album is titled *Acoustic* and is The Nitty Gritty Dirt Band's 26th album. Jeff Hanna says, "Sometimes to do something new, you have to go back to doing something you used to do, and then do it a new way. Acoustic is just us, with our own charming flaws."

Jeff Hanna is married to RCA recording artist/songwriter Matraca Berg. Jeff and Matraca wrote the band's last single, "Little Angel." Jeff has two sons, both college students. Jaime, a student in Nashville, occasionally sits in on guitar with the band, and Christopher is a freshman in Utah. Jimmie Fadden and wife Blise have a married daughter, Charlotte, and a sixteen year old, Megan. They live in Nashville, where Blise has started her own accessories business and where, in his spare time, Jimmie is building a boat. Jimmy Ibbotson is divorced, lives in Aspen, Colorado, and has three children: Jennifer, Sarah and James. Bob Carpenter married Gretchen Parsons and they live in Los Angeles with their young son, Sean.

TORTILLA SOUP IS THE REAL NITTY GRITTY

1 dried ancho chile
¼ cup olive oil
4 corn tortillas, cut into 1" pieces
1 large onion, chopped
1 medium green pepper, chopped
3 cloves garlic, minced

4 cups chicken broth
½ tsp cumin
1 Tbsp chopped parsley
2 Tbsp chopped cilantro
black pepper to taste
2 tomatoes, peeled and chopped

Remove stem and seeds from chile; sauté whole in hot oil in dutch oven until soft. Remove chile, and chop, reserving drippings in dutch oven. Fry tortilla pieces in drippings until brown. Remove and drain, reserving drippings in dutch oven. Sauté onion, green pepper and garlic in drippings until tender. Add broth, cumin and pepper.

Bring to a boil; reduce heat; simmer 20 minutes. Stir in reserved chile, tomatoes, simmer 10 minutes. Before serving, stir in cilantro and parsley. To serve, place fried tortilla pieces in individual soup bowls, reserving one fourth of chips. Add soup. Top with reserved chips.

KENNY ROGERS

Kenny Roger's track record in the music industry (after a quarter of a century) is extremely impressive: three Grammys, ten People's Choice Awards, eighteen American Music Awards, five Country Music Association Awards and eight Academy of Country Music Awards. He has nine platinum albums (six are multi-platinum), one platinum single and enough gold albums and singles to stock Fort Knox.

Although Kenny's musical honors are well deserved and appreciated, his most personal award was not bestowed upon him by the entertainment industry. In 1990, Kenny was one of eleven people (and the only entertainer) to receive the Horatio Alger Award, given to those people who have distinguished themselves despite humble beginnings. Kenny Rogers was raised in a Houston public housing project with seven brothers and sisters.

Today, he shows no signs of slowing down. New recording projects, a new stage show, TV appearances, charitable undertakings, his own clothing line and even a whole new career as a restaurateur (Kenny Rogers' Roasters—a chain of wood-roasted chicken restaurants offering a healthier alternative to fast foods) assure that he has a minimum of spare time to kill. "I think success is not a reason to quit," says Kenny. "I happen to love what I'm doing."

Dear Friends,

Good food shared with family and friends is one of the real pleasures in life. I'm on the road so much performing, recording or filming. It's really a treat to sit down and enjoy a relaxing meal. I'm pleased to share this recipe with you, it is a favorite of mine and believe me, it is meant to warm a Southern boy's heart and soul!

THE GAMBLER'S FIRE AND ICE CHILI

1 (20 oz) can pineapple chunks in syrup
1 (28 oz) can whole tomatoes, with juice
1 (6 oz) can tomato paste
1 (4 oz) can diced green chiles
3 cloves garlic, pressed or minced
2 medium yellow onions, chopped
1 green bell pepper, seeded and chopped
¼ cup chili powder

4 tsp ground cumin
1 Tbsp diced jalapeño peppers*
2 tsp salt
2 Tbsp olive oil
2 lbs lean boneless pork butt, cut into
  1" cubes

Condiments: small bowls of sliced green onions, shredded cheddar cheese and dairy sour cream

Drain pineapple, reserving syrup. Drain and chop tomatoes, reserving juice. In large bowl, combine reserved syrup, tomatoes and juice, tomato paste, green chiles, 2 cloves of garlic, 1 onion, bell pepper, chili powder, cumin, jalapeños and salt. Heat olive oil in dutch oven until very hot. Brown pork on all sides in batches. (Don't overcrowd pot. Add just enough pork to cover bottom.) With all browned pork in pot, add remaining garlic and onion. Cook until onion is soft. Add tomato mixture to pork mixture. Cover and simmer 3 hours, stirring occasionally. Add pineapple for the last 30 minutes of cooking. Serve with condiments. Serves 8 – 10.

*For more fire, add 2 Tbsp jalapeños.
Happy eating!

ROY ROGERS AND DALE EVANS

Roy Rogers and Dale Evans, the King of the Cowboys and the Queen of the Cowgirls, were married on New Year's Eve, 1947. Roy described Dale as, "my sweetheart and fishing partner all wrapped into one." They began as a family unit with Roy's three children, Cheryl, Linda and Roy, Jr. (Dusty). Roy's first wife died suddenly in 1946. Dale had a grown son from a teenage elopement, and when she and Roy married, Thomas Fox was a student at USC. It was the birth of their only child, a Downs Syndrome girl named Robin Elizabeth, that inspired Dale to write the acclaimed classic book, *Angel Unaware*. Over the years she has written 25 books.

Dale was born on October 31, 1912, in Uvalde, Texas. She was a secretary in Memphis while singing on various radio programs, finally as a staff singer on WBBM and CBS in Chicago. From Chicago she went to Hollywood to work on the *Edgar Bergen Show* where Republic Pictures heard her and signed her to a contract. She appeared in six movies the first year and then joined the Roy Rogers Western Musical Series for 26 pictures.

Roy Rogers has starred in 91 feature motion pictures and 102 TV films. He was known as the hero in the white ten-gallon hat astride his beloved palomino, Trigger. From 1943 to 1955, he was America's number one cowboy. Roy was born on November 5, 1911, in Cincinnati, Ohio. The spot where his first home stood is now second base at the Riverfront Stadium, home of the Cincinnati Reds.

Roy and Dale have adopted four children and raised one foster child—nine children in all. A Korean daughter, Debbie, lost her life on a church bus and John David (Sandy) was killed while in the U.S. armed forces in an accident in Germany. Dale and Roy have 16 grandchildren and 25 great-grandchildren. They live in Apple Valley, California, and have a personal museum in Victorville.

HAPPY TRAILS CHILI

1 can chili and beans
1 can white or yellow hominy

onions, chopped
grated cheese

In a baking dish arrange in alternate layers chili, cheese, onions and hominy, top with grated cheese and bake in a moderate 350° oven until onions are tender and cheese is thoroughly melted.

RICKY SKAGGS

Ricky Lee Skaggs was born on July 18, 1954, in Cordell, Kentucky. When he was five, his father bought him a mandolin and within two weeks he was singing and playing progressions. When he was big enough, his father gave him a guitar, and by the age of ten Ricky was mastering the fiddle. In 1961, his parents tried to get him a spot on the Grand Ole Opry but were told he was too young. In June 1982, he was inducted as the Opry's 61st member (and youngest at the time).

In 1970, Ricky joined The Clinch Mountain Boys as a mandolin player and vocalist. By the time he was nineteen, he'd tired of the long hours and low pay and decided to give up music and move to Washington, D.C. There he took a job in the boiler room of the Virginia Electric and Power Company, but abandoned it when the pull of music became too strong. He joined The Country Gentlemen as a fiddle player and then in 1975 formed his own group, Boone Creek. He began to experiment with ways to crossbreed country and bluegrass with jazz, folk and rock. It was through this circle of musicians that he met Emmylou Harris and joined her Hot Band in 1977.

Ricky moved to Nashville in 1980, where he played fiddle with The Whites. On August 4, 1981, he wed Sharon White, and they now have four children: Mandy, Andrew, Molly Kate and Lucas.

Also in 1981, he signed with Epic Records, where he's had four platinum and three gold albums. He has received Grammy awards, Academy of Country Music honors and Country Music Association awards.

RICKY'S CHICKEN PICKIN' CORN SOUP

3 or 4 chicken breasts
4 medium potatoes
2 medium onions
1 can whole kernel corn
1 can cream style corn
1 can cream of chicken soup

1 can cream of mushroom soup
5 Tbsp Wesson oil
1½ Tbsp cornstarch
1 cup water
salt & pepper
McCormick's chicken seasoning

Cut chicken into bite-sized pieces. Season with salt, pepper and chicken seasoning and brown in Wesson oil. Remove chicken from pot. Combine soups with one can water and bring to boil. Add potatoes and onions. Add whole kernel corn and cream style corn. Bring to boil and put chicken back in pot. Mix cornstarch with 1 cup water and add to soup, stirring well. Cover and simmer on medium heat 45 minutes to 1 hour. Stir occasionally to prevent sticking.

Note: This is Ricky Skaggs' original recipe that he stirred up in his own kitchen.

THE SONS OF THE PIONEERS

The Sons of the Pioneers are truly pioneers of country music. It all began in 1933, with Len Slye, Bob Nolan and Tim Spencer forming The Pioneer Trio. In 1934, when Hugh Farr joined the group, they became The Sons of the Pioneers. Following members were Karl Farr and Lloyd Perryman. In 1937, Len Slye left the group to become Roy Rogers, "King of the Cowboys," at Republic Studios. Pat Brady was his replacement, then later became Roy's sidekick and drove the jeep "Nellybelle." Bob Nolan and Tim Spencer retired in 1949, and Tom Doss and Ken Curtis replaced them. Ken left in 1952, and later played the character of Festus Hagen on the TV series *Gunsmoke*. Dale Warren took his place. That was 41 years ago, and today the group is still active under Dale's leadership.

The Sons of the Pioneers have over 3,000 compositions to their credit (including the classics "Cool Water" and "Tumbling Tumbleweeds") and have appeared in 98 motion pictures (45 with Roy Rogers). They are in music halls of fame in Arizona, Nebraska, Oklahoma, Tennessee and Texas. They were designated "National Treasures" by the Smithsonian Institution in Washington, D.C., have a star on Hollywood's Walk of Fame and today are preparing to lay down the vocals for their 60th anniversary album.

SERVE TUCSON LENTIL SOUP WITH COOL WATER

1½ cups dried lentils, soaked overnight
1 quart cold water
1 small onion, chopped
½ bell pepper, chopped
1 small carrot, finely diced
1 large clove of garlic, minced
2 Tbsp canned green chiles, chopped

½ cup tomato paste or 1 (6 oz) can
   tomato sauce
2 small chicken bouillon cubes
1 small dried red pepper pod or ¼ tsp
   dried red pepper flakes
1 pinch dry sweet basil
1 small bay leaf

Into large pot add lentils and bouillon cubes to quart of cold water. Cook on medium heat for 50 minutes. Add more water as needed, keeping lentils just covered. While lentils are cooking, sauté in a non-stick skillet: onion, bell pepper, carrot and garlic until soft, then add remaining ingredients. Add skillet mixture to lentils and cook until lentils are tender. Remove from heat and cool. Remove bay leaf and puree soup in a blender until smooth. To serve, reheat and top soup with a dollop of light sour cream.

SWEETHEARTS OF THE RODEO

Sweethearts of the Rodeo, sisters Kristine Oliver Arnold and Janis Oliver (Mrs. Vince) Gill, are celebrating their thirteenth year of singing together. Growing up in Manhattan Beach, California, they became interested in music before they were teenagers, listening to their older brothers' records. Janis was just learning to play the guitar, and the influences of Sonny Terry and Brownie McGhee, Doc Watson, John Lee Hooker and Bill Monroe had a great effect on her. Soon Kristine began singing to Janis's accompaniment and harmonies and by the time they started high school they'd organized a bluegrass/folk band. They spent years on the Southern California club circuit before signing with a major record label, with both girls getting married along the way.

They recorded four albums for Columbia: *Sweethearts of the Rodeo* (which included five Top 20 hits), *One Time One Night, Buffalo Zone* and *Sisters*. Their career is filled with an impressive list of nominations including the Country Music Association's Vocal Duo and Horizon awards as well as *Music City News'* Vocal Duo and TNN's Viewer's Choice Favorite Group award. The sisters recently signed with Sugar Hill Records and have just completed their first album for that label titled *Rodeo Waltz*. Janis Gill produced the album and shared acoustic guitar roles with her husband Vince. "He's an incredible rhythm guitarist as well as lead," says Janis. "I really wanted the benefit of that on this album. I would find one part and then he'd find another and complement what I was playing. It was just the greatest feeling in the world."

THE SISTERS' TURKEY CHILI

1 lb ground turkey
1 medium onion, chopped
1 medium green pepper, chopped
2 cloves garlic, minced
vegetable cooking spray
3 (14 oz) cans stewed tomatoes, drained and chopped

2 (15 oz) cans pinto beans, drained
⅔ cup salsa or picante sauce
1 Tbsp chili powder
1 Tbsp ground cumin
¼ tsp ground red pepper
1 Tbsp sugar

Spray pot with cooking spray. Sauté onion, garlic and green pepper. Add turkey and cook until crumbly. Add rest of ingredients and simmer for 30 minutes. Serve with chopped onion, shredded cheese and sour cream. For spicier chili, turn the heat up with added red pepper. This supplies the "fire" in this recipe.

91

MEL TILLIS

Mel Tillis was born Lonnie Melvin Tillis on August 8, 1932, in Tampa, Florida. He was in the U.S. Air Force from 1951 to 1955, and it was while stationed in Okinawa that Mel got his first paid job as a musician. He joined a band (The Westerners) and entertained weekends and evenings in local military clubs.

Before becoming a country music legend, Mel worked in Florida as a strawberry picker, a milkman and a fireman on the Atlantic Coast Line Railroad. He signed his first recording contract in 1956. In 1957 he made a permanent move to Nashville as an independent songwriter who also played guitar for such country greats as Minnie Pearl.

Not only is Mel an incredible songwriter (1976 Nashville Songwriters Association International Hall of Fame) and an amazing entertainer (1976 Country Music Association's Entertainer of the Year) but he has appeared in films such as *Every Which Way But Loose* with Clint Eastwood and *Smokey And The Bandit II* with Burt Reynolds.

Mel says a question he's asked most is: "How did you begin stuttering?" "Well, it happened right after I had malaria when I was about three," says Mel. "I also had a friend named LeRoy English who stuttered, and I honestly don't know whether I started stuttering from the malaria or from being around LeRoy so much."

Today Mel works from April through October at his Mel Tillis Ozark Theatre in Branson, Missouri. He performs an additional forty days per year throughout the country.

I BELIEVE IN YOU AND HAMBURGER STEW

2 lbs ground beef
4 – 5 large carrots, sliced thin
3 – 4 large potatoes, cubed
1 large onion, chopped

1 pkg frozen or 9 – 10 fresh pods okra,
  chopped
salt
pepper

Brown beef in a skillet, drain off excess grease. Put ground beef in a large pot and add chopped onion, potatoes, carrots, salt and pepper. Cover ingredients with water and cook with lid on for 30 minutes. Add okra. Cover and cook an additional 15 minutes. You may have to add water while cooking. Serve over rice. Serves 6.

TRAVIS TRITT

Travis Tritt describes his story as a case of "overnight success that took eight and a half years to happen." Born and raised in Marietta, Georgia, he followed the classic country road of having begun his musical career as a soloist in the children's choir at the neighborhood church. He taught himself to play the guitar at the age of eight and wrote his first song when he was only fourteen.

Upon graduation from high school in 1981, Travis went to work loading trucks and within four years had worked his way up to a management position. But he kept wondering if he had the talent to make it in country music. Finally, he quit his job and began playing solo at any club that would have him. Before long, he came to the attention of Danny Davenport, a local representative for Warner Brothers Records. At first Danny's interest in Travis was simply as a songwriter. But once he started watching him perform he knew there could be more. Together they began working on an album in Danny's home studio. Two years later they took it to Warner Brothers and the rest is history.

Today, Travis continues to barnstorm the concert circuit with as much crowd-pleasing energy as ever. In 1992, he was inducted into the Opry and currently resides as the youngest member. Travis recently defined his love for country music: "To me, country music is a soundtrack for the lives of working people."

HELP ME HOLD ON TO HOT AND SPICY CHILI

1 lb ground beef
2 cans New Orleans style kidney beans, drained
2 (14 oz) cans stewed tomatoes
1 small can tomato paste
1 (12 oz) can Budweiser beer
1 large bell pepper, chopped coarsely
1 medium white onion, chopped coarsely

2 Tbsp hot chili powder
½ tsp minced garlic
3 Tbsp yellow mustard
2 Tbsp sweet basil
½ tsp oregano
2 jalapeño peppers, sliced
Lawry's Hot 'n Spicy Seasoned Salt to taste

Brown ground beef, drain and transfer to crock pot. Add remaining ingredients and mix well. Cook on low 8 – 10 hours or on high 3 – 4 hours. Cover with your favorite shredded cheese and Tabasco to taste and enjoy.

P.S. Have plenty of Pepto-Bismol on hand.

95

JERRY JEFF WALKER

Jerry Jeff Walker has outlasted nickel Cokes, the Berlin Wall and six Presidents (and the current one is a big fan, as is Texas Governor Ann Richards). For over a quarter-century, he has enjoyed success as a musician, a singer and a songwriter. As the composer of scores of songs, including the classic "Mr. Bojangles," Jerry Jeff has 24 albums to his credit. His latest, *Viva Luckenbach!*, was released in March 1994. It is his second album to be released on his own label that he and his wife Susan formed in 1986. The label, Tried And True Music, boasts Susan as "president, manager and booking agent" and Jerry Jeff as "talent pool, creative centerpiece and chief cook and bottle washer." Their first effort, *Gypsy Songman*, was recorded mostly in their den.

Jerry Jeff's career began in 1967, with the short-lived "psychedelic folk/rock" group called Circus Maximus. Then came his phenomenal success with "Mr. Bojangles" in 1968. He moved to Austin, Texas, in 1971 and has remained a resident of the Lone Star State for over 23 years along with his wife Susan and their two children, Django and Jessie.

In 1993, he managed to play for both Governor Ann Richards' and President Bill Clinton's inaugurations, tour Europe and the Caribbean and...turn 50!

MR. BOJANGLE'S CORN CHOWDER

1 large potato, peeled and diced
1 (18 oz) can chicken broth
2 Tbsp butter
1 onion, chopped
2 Tbsp flour
2 cups sweet corn (fresh or frozen)

1 (2 – 4 oz) can diced green chilis
1 quart milk
granulated garlic
salt
pepper

In medium saucepan, simmer the potato in the broth with salt until tender. Heat the butter in a frying pan and sauté the onion until tender. Stir in flour, blend well and continue to sauté stirring for another 2 – 3 minutes. Add this to the potato in its liquid and bring to a simmer. Reduce heat and add the corn, chilis (according to your taste for spicy-hot!), milk and seasonings. bring to a gentle simmer—don't let it boil—then cover and cook for 20 minutes. Add salt and pepper to taste.

HANK WILLIAMS, JR.

The son of country music's first superstar, Randall Hank Williams ("Bocephus" was his late father's nickname for him) was born May 26, 1949, just one month before Hank, Sr.'s landmark first appearance on the Grand Ole Opry. Hank Williams, Jr. made his first appearance on the Opry at age eleven, and at fourteen he made his first record. A year later he sang the soundtrack of *Your Cheatin' Heart*, Hank Sr.'s film biography.

His teen years were by no means ordinary. Instead of playing Little League baseball, he was learning to play the piano from Jerry Lee Lewis. In high school, he'd grown weary of being a "Hank Williams clone," and began playing contemporary rock music as "Rockin' Randall." Then came drug and alcohol abuse and a 1974 suicide attempt. A different Hank, Jr. emerged from the psychological ashes. He pulled back, sized up the musical landscape, looked deep into his soul and found the Hank, Jr. we now know.

While mountain climbing with friends on Ajax Mountain on the Montana/Idaho border, he took a 500-foot fall that caused severe injuries to his head and face. With a good deal of reconstructive surgery yet to be done, he hit the road to perform. His career now boasts 63 albums, including ten number-one singles and fourteen number-one, 20 gold and five platinum albums.

Hank, Jr., his wife Mary Jane and their daughter Katherine divide their time between their recently completed plantation-style mansion in the wilds of Montana, and Tennessee, where Hank has an office complex that handles, among other things, a 20,000-member fan club. The legend's son has forged his own legend.

98

COWPUNCHER'S STEW

1½ lbs stew meat, cut in 2" pieces
2 Tbsp flour
1 tsp salt
2 Tbsp shortening
1½ cups strong coffee
2 Tbsp molasses
1 clove garlic, minced
1 tsp worcestershire sauce

½ tsp crushed oregano
⅛ tsp cayenne
1½ cups water
4 carrots, cut in ½" slices
4 onions, quartered
3 potatoes, peeled and cut up
¼ cup cold water
3 Tbsp flour

Coat meat with a mixture of 2 Tbsp flour and 1 tsp salt. In a dutch oven, brown meat on all sides in shortening. Stir in coffee, molasses, garlic, 1 tsp salt, worcestershire, oregano and cayenne. Cover and simmer on low heat about 1½ hours. Add 1½ cups water, carrots, onions and potatoes. Simmer for 30 minutes, until vegetables are tender. Blend 3 Tbsp flour into ¼ cup cold water. Add to stew mixture. Cook and stir until thickened a bit.

ENTREES & SIDE DISHES

BILL ANDERSON

"Whisperin' Bill" (a nickname hung on him because of his breathy voice) Anderson was born in Columbia, South Carolina, and grew up around Atlanta, Georgia. He graduated from the University of Georgia with a degree in journalism, but was performing and writing songs while still in school. He was nineteen when he composed the country classic "City Lights."

Bill moved to Nashville, secured a recording contract with Decca and began turning out hit after hit with songs like "Po' Folks," "Mama Sang A Song," "The Tips Of My Fingers," "8 X 10" and the country and pop smash "Still." His compositions have been recorded by such diverse musical talents as Ray Price, Porter Wagoner, Debbie Reynolds, Ivory Joe Hunter, Kitty Wells, Faron Young, Lawrence Welk, Dean Martin, Aretha Franklin, Jerry Lee Lewis and Walter Brennan. In 1975, he was inducted into the Nashville Songwriters Hall of Fame and in 1985, the State of Georgia chose him as the seventh living performer to be inducted into the Georgia Music Hall of Fame.

He was the first country artist to host a network game show (ABC's *The Better Sex*) and appeared for three years on the daytime soap *One Life To Live*. His autobiography, *Whisperin' Bill*, was published by Longstreet Press in 1989 and is now in its fourth printing. His second book, a humorous look at the music business, titled *I Hope You're Living As High On The Hog As The Pig You Turned Out To Be*, was published in 1993. Bill lives in Nashville where he has been a member of the Grand Ole Opry since 1961. He currently hosts the popular *Opry Backstage* TV show 26 Saturday nights a year and records for Curb Records.

WHISPERING BILL'S GOOD ENOUGH TO SHOUT ABOUT THREE BEAN CASSEROLE

1 (10 oz) pkg frozen lima beans
1 (10 oz) pkg frozen green peas

1 (10 oz) pkg frozen green beans

Cook on full boil for 20 minutes with salt added. Drain well. Mix with sauce below.

Sauce

1½ cups mayonnaise
1 medium onion, chopped

1¼ Tbsp worchestershire sauce
3 hard boiled eggs, chopped.

Mix well.

CLINT BLACK & LISA HARTMAN BLACK

Clint Black and Lisa Hartman Black were both born in Houston, Texas. It was also in Houston that they met for the first time on New Year's Eve, 1990, when Lisa and her mother (publicist Jonni Hartman) went to see Clint in concert at Houston's Summit Arena. Their first date occurred a few weeks later when Clint came to Los Angeles and gave her a call. They were married on October 2, 1991, on a small farm near Houston with only their families attending the wedding. They are still on their honeymoon.

Country music superstar Clint Black has written or co-written every song on each of his four platinum and multi-platinum RCA albums. Beginning with his 1989 debut album, *Killin' Time*, he scored ten number-one singles. He was honored with the Country Music Association's Horizon Award in 1989 and Male Vocalist award in 1990. The Nashville Songwriters Association International presented him with the organization's first Songwriter/Artist of the Year award. His fourth album for RCA, *No Time To Kill*, has already yielded four hits.

Lisa Hartman Black made television history as the only prime-time TV character to be killed off one season and brought back by popular demand to the same series as someone else.

The "reincarnated" Lisa moved from Ciji Dunne to Cathy Geary on the popular and long-running *Knots Landing*. She has gone on to star in a number of movies-of-the-week and multi-hour miniseries. Lisa grew up in the theatre and moved to Los Angeles from Houston to star in her first TV series *Tabitha*, a spin-off from *Bewitched*.

Lisa and Clint make their homes in Los Angeles and Nashville.

CLINT & LISA'S GUILTLESS BURRITOS

Corn tortillas or lowfat flour tortillas
broiled or baked skinless, boneless chicken
   breasts, shredded
chopped lettuce
chopped tomato

salsa
spicy black bean dip (Guiltless Gourmet
   brand is a must because it is FAT FREE
   and delicious)
fat-free sour cream (optional)

Load all ingredients into tortillas; roll. Devour and enjoy with no guilt!!!!!!

105

SUZY BOGGUSS

Suzy Bogguss is currently enjoying the satisfaction that comes from directing her multifaceted career during such an exciting period of growth for country music. In 1991, she received a Grammy nomination for "Hopelessly Yours," a duet with Lee Greenwood. In 1992, she won the Country Music Association's Horizon Award, presented to the best new talent, and her album *Aces* was certified gold. She was also named the Academy of Country Music's Top New Female Vocalist.

Suzy graduated from Illinois State University with a major in metal-smithing. She moved to Nashville in 1985 following a lengthy solo performance tour of the United States and Mexico, where she booked herself into clubs. Her first jobs in Music City were singing at a restaurant and doing some demo work. Later, she signed to perform at Dollywood, and it was there that she was discovered by Liberty Records.

Suzy has not been content to confine her activities to the recording studio or to touring. (In 1993, she played a sold-out tour schedule with Dwight Yoakam.) Her fashion designs and leather clothing line are carried in upscale stores such as Nordstrom, and she strives to satisfy the consumer in herself. "It's like when you go to the store and say, 'Now if this coat only had that collar, I'd buy it.' Now I can put together all the pieces I like. That's how I put things together when I make an album."

HEY, CINDERELLA, HAVE SOME FRITTATA

½ cup butter
5 eggs
1 cup Bisquick
1 cup milk

1 lb Monterey Jack cheese, grated
2 pkgs frozen, chopped spinach, thawed
  and thoroughly drained

Melt butter in a 7" X 11" baking dish. In a separate bowl, beat eggs and add Bisquick, milk, cheese and spinach. Pour mixture into baking dish with butter, and bake 35 – 40 minutes at 350°. Let cool and serve with salsa!

BOY HOWDY

Larry Park, founder of the group Boy Howdy explains their name: "To us, the name's like a celebration of country music. 'Boy, howdy.' In the old western movies, you'd see somebody riding off on a horse and they'd say, 'Boy, howdy, did you see that guy shoot that gun?' That kind of thing. It's a very western expression." Well, a long list of musicians rode off into the sunset before Larry found a line-up for the band that pleased him: Cary Park, Jeffrey Steele and Hugh Wright. Each of the four band members spent a minimum of ten years playing "brutal club dates" before Boy Howdy solidified.

The band is extremely close. Last year, drummer Hugh Wright was hit by a car while trying to help a roadside accident victim. After receiving the news of his life-threatening injuries, the other three members pondered the future of the band. Cary remembers, "We were deciding what we were going to do. 'Should we break this thing up, or continue?' We decided, 'No, we worked too hard. We're gonna keep it going for Hugh to have something to come back to.'" Continuous tapes, phone calls, letters and support from the rest of the band on the road helped pull Hugh through a five-month coma.

Jeffrey Steel says, "We're country to the bone, and we grew up with that whole Bakersfield sound." Larry adds, "We've always known what parts to sing. We never have to sit down and work them out—it's just a natural thing."

SHE'D GIVE ANYTHING FOR BARBEQUED CHICKEN BREASTS

6 skinned chicken breasts
Chef Paul Prudhomme's Magic Seasoning
  Blend's Redfish Magic

Billy Blue's Smoky Pecan Barbeque Sauce
garlic powder
ground pepper

Sprinkle Redfish Magic Seasoning, garlic powder and ground pepper to taste on both sides of each breast and pat down. Put on the fire at a very low heat and cook for about 40 – 45 minutes. When chicken is done and while it is still on grill, use a brush to dab each piece with barbeque sauce. Let sauce just reach the temperature of the chicken. Serve and enjoy!

BROOKS AND DUNN

Recent Grammy winners Brooks and Dunn are Leon Eric Brooks III (but he's been called Kix all of his life), born in Shreveport, Louisiana, and Ronnie Gene Dunn, born in Coleman, Texas, but raised in Tulsa, Oklahoma. Ronnie grew up performing in his dad's band in west Texas, while Kix did his first "paying gig" at the age of twelve—playing at Johnny Horton's daughter's birthday party!

Ronnie and Kix met just a few months before their career caught fire. Ronnie had come to Nashville from Oklahoma for the finals of the Marlboro National Talent Round-up (which he won) and their chemistry was instantaneous. He'd been involved with some people surrounding Leon Russell's Shelter Records and became part of the region's thriving country scene while Kix was "seriously honky-tonking" in college. Kix moved to Nashville and got his first break as a songwriter with a cut on The Oak Ridge Boys' million-selling *Bobbie Sue*.

Brooks and Dunn released their first album, *Brand New Man*, and it became the most successful debut album ever released by a country duo or group. It spawned four straight number-one singles and sold nearly three million copies. It also earned them a Grammy nomination for Best Performance by a Duo or Group in the Country category.

Kix Brooks is married to Barbara and they have two children, Molly and Eric. In his spare time, he enjoys playing golf and shooting pool. Ronnie Dunn is married to Janine and they also have two children, Whitney and Jesse. Ronnie collects cowboy paraphernalia.

PORK CHOPS AND SAUERKRAUT WILL MAKE YOU FEEL LIKE A BRAND NEW MAN

4 butterfly pork chops
¼ cup butter
½ small onion, chopped

Cavender's seasoning mix, to taste
1 jar Vlasic sauerkraut

Season pork chops generously with Cavender's and pepper. Sauté pork chops and onion together until brown. Add sauerkraut (partially drain liquid), and simmer for one to two hours. Serve with mashed potatoes and vegetables of your choice.

111

CARLENE CARTER

Carlene Carter has an amazing family tree. She is the granddaughter of Mother Maybelle Carter of the original Carter Family, daughter of June Carter Cash and Carl Smith and stepdaughter of Johnny Cash. Carlene began her career as a

songwriter. When she was 21, she co-wrote "Easy From Now On" for Emmylou Harris. In the 1980s, while living in England, her songs were recorded by Tracy Nelson, The Go-Go's and The Doobie Brothers.

In the mid-80s, she returned to the United States and moved back into her family's home in Tennessee and abandoned her fast-lane lifestyle. She joined her mother and her aunts, Helen and Anita, for a two-year stint on the road and the recording of the 1988 album *Wildwood Flower*. "I wanted to know about the Carter Family music," she says. "They were pioneers who influenced a lot of people."

Then her 1990 first solo country album, *I Fell In Love*, was released. She received a Grammy nomination in 1991 for Country Female Performance for that album, and also an Academy of Country Music nomination for Best New Female Vocalist that same year. Her current album, *Little Love Letters*, is her second album produced by her boyfriend Howie Epstein (of Tom Petty's Heartbreakers) for Giant Records.

I FELL IN LOVE WITH ANGEL HAIR PASTA WITH WHITE CLAM SAUCE

I am a short-cut kinda cook in that I never really measure anything and I jam when I cook. In other words I do it by instinct and taste. It's like writing a song to me.

First off you need fresh angel hair pasta, the kind that cooks in 3 – 4 minutes.
½ stick butter
approximately 4 Tbsp olive oil
1 small onion, chopped
½ clove garlic, chopped
garlic powder

Italian seasoning, such as oregano, basil, salt and pepper, to taste
6 medium mushrooms, chopped
1 can minced or chopped clams, depending on your preference
6 oz cream cheese
water if needed for consistency control

First start your water to boil (you won't need to put the pasta in until the sauce is done); put butter in water. Put olive oil in skillet, heat to medium-low. Add chopped onions, mushrooms, garlic and seasonings to taste; cook till onions are transparent. Add clams and cook for about a minute. Mix all ingredients around in the skillet. Add cream cheese and mix till it's the right consistency(smooth); if needed you can add a little water or more cream cheese. Stir and simmer for about 5 – 7 minutes. Then you're ready to make the pasta. I like to make some garlic bread while the pasta is cooking. When pasta is ready, drain and add sauce. Serve with caesar salad and garlic bread. Parmesan cheese optional. This is a great meal in a very short preparation time—approximately 20 minutes if you jam! P.S. For red clam sauce, substitute tomato sauce and chopped tomatoes for cream cheese.

Love and enjoy,
CARLENE

DIAMOND RIO

Six world-class talents make up Diamond Rio: lead vocalist Marty Roe; lead guitarist Jimmy Olander; keyboardist Dan Truman; fiddler, mandolinist and vocalist Gene Johnson; bass player and vocalist Dana Williams and drummer Brian Prout.

After playing in a number of country bands, Marty joined The Tennessee River Boys, which would evolve into Diamond Rio in 1984. Brian's background included stints in both country and rock groups. Gene had played with the likes of David Bromberg and J. D. Crowe. Jimmy Olander played with the Dirt Band, Rodney Crowell and Duanne Eddy, while Dana had worked with Vassar Clements and Jimmy C. Newman. Dan Truman is a classically taught pianist with jazz leanings. The result has been an impressive set of accomplishments. Their first album, *Diamond Rio*, is nearing platinum status.

In 1991, they were the Academy of Country Music's Top Vocal Group as well as the Country Music Association's Vocal Group of the Year. They have achieved widespread popular appeal, releasing hit after hit to a rapidly growing fan base while maintaining a level of musical sophistication that continues to set them apart. The mix of influences and the emphasis on arrangements and musicianship grow out of one of the band's main strengths: the long and varied backgrounds of its members. "We've got three guys that grew up playing bluegrass, a guy who was a rock n' roller, one with a jazz background and one who's traditional country," says Jimmy Olander. "Throw that all together and you've got a unique sound."

Rio Good Beef n' Stout

1 Tbsp of butter
1 Tbsp of corn oil
2 lbs top round steak cut into 2" cubes
4 medium onions, sliced
2 cups mushroom buttons, halved

2 Tbsp flour
¼ cup stout (dark beer)
1 bay leaf
1 tsp dark brown sugar
salt and pepper to taste

Heat butter and oil in large dutch oven and cook meat for 10 minutes or until brown. Remove meat from pot with slotted spoon. Add onions and mushrooms and fry for 5 minutes or until they are softened. Season with salt and pepper to taste. Add flour and stir well so flour absorbs fat. Return the meat to the pan and pour in the stout. Add the bay leaf and brown sugar. Stir well to mix. Cover and cook gently on the stovetop on low heat or place in the oven at 300° for 2½ hours. Make sure that meat is tender. Serves 4 – 6. Serve with hot crusty German rye bread and sautéd carrots and zucchini sticks.

THIS IS ONE OF GENE JOHNSON'S FAVORITE RECIPES!!!

115

JOE ELY

When Joe Ely was seven years old, his parents took him to a local Pontiac dealership in Amarillo, Texas, to hear a singer named Jerry Lee Lewis. It was something he'd never forget. "You could hardly see across the street, and then there's this madman up there pounding on a piano. The wind was blowing so hard that it would blow the microphone over. Jerry Lee would be singing and the microphone would go thump! And somebody'd run over and pick it up and it would fall over again. It was like a vision from hell. But it was so wonderful because it seemed like it fit, with the wind and the static electricity in the air. I always look back at that moment as the very beginning, the spark that made me consider doing this as my life."

Before Joe finished high school, he was on the road with his guitar. "I had been reading a lot of Jack Kerouac and Henry Miller and listening to Woody Guthrie songs," he says. "I started tracing the routes of these legendary guys. I spent a few years doing that, just jumping freight trains."

In 1977, he signed with MCA. His debut album, *Joe Ely*, was followed by *Honky*

Tonk Masquerade (listed by *Rolling Stone* magazine as one of the top albums of the 70s). In 1990, he returned to MCA (after having several successes at Hightone Records) to record *Live At Liberty Lunch*. In 1991, four of his early MCA albums were remastered and made available on CD for the first time: *Joe Ely, Honky Tonk Masquerade, Down On The Drag* and *Musta Notta Gotta Lotta*. His current album, *Love and Danger*, signals the beginning of a new Joe Ely era.

MUSTA NOTTA GOTTA LOTTA POSOLE

2 quarts water
3 – 5 Tbsp Herb-Ox chicken bouillon
2 – 2½ lbs pork roast
2 large cans white hominy
2 small cans yellow hominy

1 large can whole tomatoes
2 cups roasted green chiles, fresh
lots of oregano
4 large cloves garlic, fresh

Boil water, then add bouillon. Cut pork into small cubes and set aside. Throw bone into broth for 10 – 15 minutes; remove bone. Add pork and hominy to broth. Drain canned tomatoes, chop and add to broth. Add minced green chiles, then garlic and oregano to taste. Boil until pork is done (about 40 minutes). It should be very thick; add more water as it boils off. Eat and enjoy!!!

117

EVANGELINE

Evangeline started in 1988 when Rhonda Lohmeyer, Kathleen Stieffel, Sharon Leger and Beth McKee united with the goal of creating original country music with all-female harmonies. They took their name from that most famous Louisiana woman—the long lost lover from Longfellow's epic poem about the migration of Acadians from Nova Scotia to Louisiana.

Each member of Evangeline contributes her own special musical elements to the band. Bass and washboard player Sharon Leger comes from Cajun country in central Louisiana and worked on several albums by Cajun artist Bruce Daigrepont. Keyboardist Beth McKee is from Jackson, Mississippi, and is a veteran of the Austin blues scene and The Fingers Taylor Band. Lead guitarist Rhonda Lohmeyer has a country and country-rock background and guitarist Kathleen Stieffel, from Bay St. Louis (on the Gulf Coast about an hour from New Orleans), also came up in country bands.

In their beginning in 1988, they landed a job at a Bourbon Street club and entered the first ever Jazz Search, a talent contest sponsored by the New Orleans Jazz and Heritage Festival. They won first place. They went on to win two country music contests, the Marlboro Talent Roundup and the True Value Country Music Showdown. This brought them to the attention of Margaritaville Records and the release of their first album.

Don't Cross That Bridge Without Southern Chicken Bog

1 3½ – 4 lb chicken, cut up
5½ cups water
1 tsp poultry seasoning
1 cup onion, chopped
½ cup celery, chopped

½ lb low-fat turkey kielbasa sausage, cut
   into ½" slices
2 cups uncooked rice
salt & pepper to taste
1 (2 oz) jar sliced pimentos, drained

Place chicken in a 4-quart casserole. Add water and poultry seasoning. Cover with lid and microwave on high 30 minutes. Remove chicken to a platter to cool. Skim and discard fat from broth. Reserve 5 cups broth. Put onion and celery into same casserole; re-cover. Microwave on high 4 minutes; set aside.

Place sausage on a paper towel-lined plate and microwave on high 3 – 4 minutes. Add sausage, rice, salt, pepper and reserved broth to casserole. Cover and microwave on high 10 minutes; then microwave on medium 15 minutes.

Meanwhile, debone chicken, discarding skin, bones and fat. Cut meat into bite-sized pieces. When rice is done, add chicken and pimentos; stir.

JANIE FRICKE

Since stepping from the background as a successful jingle and session singer and into the spotlight, Janie Fricke's clear, pure voice has helped define country music. Growing up on a farm near South Whitley, Indiana, music was an integral part of her life. Her mother played piano and organ in church, and her father played guitar.

Janie parlayed her childhood love of singing into professional aspirations when she took a summer job singing radio identification jingles during college. She had been singing at coffeehouses near Indiana University, but working in the studio taught her a lot about utilizing her voice.

After obtaining her teaching degree, Janie decided to follow her heart and pursue a career in music. She worked in Memphis, Dallas and Los Angeles before settling in Nashville in 1975. She was soon one of the most sought after studio singers in Music City, singing on the records of Elvis Presley, Barbara Mandrell, Crystal Gayle, Ronnie Milsap, Mel Tillis, England Dan and John Ford Coley, Eddie Rabbitt and Johnny Duncan. Her voice was heard on numerous commercial jingles for products including 7-Up, Coca-Cola, Pizza Hut, United Airlines, Red Lobster and Coors Beer.

It was inevitable that she would eventually be offered a recording contract. Since signing with CBS Records, she has released 37 singles and 21 albums. She's been named Top New Female Vocalist by *Billboard*, *Cash Box* and the readers of *Music City News*. She was named Female Vocalist of the Year by the Country Music Association for two consecutive years, as well as receiving Top Female Vocalist honors from *Music City News*, *Billboard*, *Cash Box* and the Academy of Country Music. She was also Top Female Vocalist in Europe.

EASY TO PLEASE GREEN CHILE QUICHE

2 medium zucchini, shredded (squeeze out excess water)
2 finely chopped green onions
¼ cup canned green chiles, chopped
4 egg whites, beaten
2 eggs or egg substitute

1 cup grated part skim mozzarella
1 cup grated cheddar cheese
1½ cups evaporated skim milk
vegetable coating spray
9" pie crust (optional)

Sauté zucchini and onion in a nonstick skillet over low heat, until tender. Add water if squash begins to stick. Mix all ingredients and pour into 9" pie pan sprayed with vegetable coating spray or into pie crust. Bake at 350° until firm and lightly browned. Serves 8.

121

CRYSTAL GAYLE

The youngest of eight children, Crystal Gayle grew up singing along with the radio, always encouraged by her sister, Loretta Lynn. While in high school, Crystal signed her first recording contract. Her debut single, "I've Cried The Blue Right Out Of My Eyes" (written by Loretta), reached the Top 25 on the country charts. It was in 1974 that she had her first Top 10 hit with "Wrong Road Again." Her albums *Crystal Gayle, Somebody Loves You* and *Crystal* all made their mark on country music. Her platinum-selling albums *We Must Believe In Magic* and *When I Dream* yielded a string of hit singles including "I'll Get Over You" (her first number-one hit) and the smash crossovers "Don't It Make My Brown Eyes Blue" and "Talking In Your Sleep."

In 1982, Crystal recorded her first-ever duet, the chart-topping "You And I" with Eddie Rabbitt. She had a string of hit albums including *Cage Of The Songbird, Nobody's Angel, Ain't Gonna Worry, Three Good Reasons* and *Best Always.* She also recorded her popular Christmas album, *A Crystal Christmas* and a duet album with Gary Morris, *What If We Fall In Love,* which included the hit singles "Makin' Up For Lost Time" and "Another World" (the theme song from the hit TV soap opera).

Crystal has a shelf full of awards including a Grammy, four Academy of Country Music awards, two Country Music Association awards and three American Music Awards. She continues to perform over 100 concerts a year and spends her personal time raising her children, Catherine and Chris. She also has a business, Crystal's For Fine Gifts and Jewelry, in Nashville.

WHEN I DREAM, I DREAM OF ROAST CHICKEN AND POTATOES

whole fryer or pieces of fryer chicken,
  cleaned and washed
1 (15 oz) can Hunts Tomato Sauce
2 – 3 Tbsp olive oil

water
salt & pepper
ground cinnamon
4 – 5 potatoes, quartered

Place chicken in roasting pan. Add tomato sauce, putting some on the chicken, olive oil and enough water to fill the pan 1" deep. Sprinkle salt, pepper and cinnamon on chicken and sauce. Bake at 350°, basting once in a while. Cook until done (1 hour according to weight). Cover with foil if browning too much. Remove chicken from roasting pan, leave sauce in pan. Place chicken on a plate and set aside. Put potatoes in pan. Sprinkle with salt, pepper and cinnamon. If needed, add water to sauce in pan so that potatoes are almost covered. Cook for one hour. Stir once or twice during cooking time. Serve with cornbread (not sweet).

GEORGE JONES

George Jones is approaching the 40th anniversary of his first hit and is inarguably the greatest country singer alive. The most incredible aspect of George Jones's career is that he's still moving forward with his artistry. His most recent award was not for something he did ten or twenty years ago, it was for his latest hit, "I Don't Need Your Rockin' Chair," which won the Country Music Association's Vocal Event award for 1993.

George Glenn Jones was born and raised in the Big Thicket area of east Texas. After a stint in the Marines, he began his recording career in 1953 and scored his first hit with "Why, Baby, Why." He sang the number-one country song of all time, "He Stopped Loving Her Today." He was the Country Music Association's Best Male Vocalist in 1962 and 1963 and again in 1980 and 1981. In 1986, he won CMA's Video of the Year award with "Who's Gonna Fill Their Shoes," and in 1992, he was elected to the Country Music Hall of Fame. In his acceptance speech he asked radio programmers to give a fair chance to the older country artists.

George's life has often been likened to a country song. But his famous stormy relationships and bouts with the bottle are in the past now. He works well over 100 dates a year and the "No Show" sign on the front bumper of his tour bus is just a joking reminder of days past— he hasn't missed a show in years. When he's not performing or recording, he lives a quiet life in the Nashville suburb of Brentwood on his 70-acre farm where he has an autobiography in the works.

YOU'LL NEVER STOP LOVING CHICKEN BREASTS AND VEGGIES

chicken breasts
chopped carrots
chopped celery
chopped onions
canned or frozen whole kernel corn

canned or frozen English peas
chopped potatoes
garlic powder to taste
chicken bouillon (canned)

Combine chicken breasts, carrots, celery, onions, corn, peas, potatoes, garlic powder and bouillon in large dutch oven; mix well. Add enough water to cover. Bake at 300° for 2 hours, stirring occasionally. Serve with hot corn bread.

MCBRIDE & THE RIDE

Since being signed to MCA Nashville in 1989, McBride & The Ride have garnered two Academy of Country Music nominations for Vocal Group and two nominations for the Country Music Association's Vocal Group of the Year. *Cashbox* magazine also named them Top New Group of 1991. With the addition of three new band members at the end of 1993, the group, together, has more than 30 years of musical experience.

Joining Terry McBride and current members Gary Morse (steel guitar) and Jeffrey Roach (keyboards) are Keith Edwards (drums), Kenny Vaughan (guitar) and Randy Frazier (bass). Keith joins the band after years with Ricky Skaggs, Kenny most recently toured with Patty Loveless and Randy is a former member of Palomino Road. Ray Herndon left the group to go solo and Billy Thomas opted to go his separate way.

Terry McBride, who is the only remaining original member, was born in Austin, Texas, and grew up 60 miles up the road in Lampasas. He started playing guitar at the age of nine. After high school, he spent three years on the road with his late father, Dale

McBride, who had eleven hit records on independent labels. Eventually, Terry began to concentrate on his songwriting and making regular trips to Nashville to pitch his material.

McBride & The Ride make their film debut in the motion picture 8 *Seconds To Glory*, a rodeo film based on real-life cowboy Lane Frost, played by Luke Perry. Also making guest appearances in the film are Vince Gill and Brooks and Dunn. McBride & The Ride are also riding the crest of a number-one single from their *Sacred Ground* album and a series of Top 5 hits from their current release, *Hurry Sundown*.

AFTER SUNDOWN WE'LL HAVE MEXICAN SALAD

iceberg lettuce
pinto beans
diced tomatoes
small size Fritos

shredded cheddar cheese
Catalina dressing

Mix and toss all ingredients.

LEE ROY PARNELL

Lee Roy Parnell was raised in west Texas. When he was a young boy, the legendary western-swing originator, Bob Wills, was a close family friend and he and his band, The Texas Playboys, were frequent visitors at the Parnell home. Bob Wills and his music had a big effect on the young Lee Roy. Then, when he was a teenager, he would go to the bars in Fort Worth. It was in these clubs that he first experienced the unique mix of black and white musical styles that would also influence him.

Lee Roy arrived in Nashville in 1987. He had with him one hundred songs that he'd written and so far has not recorded one of them. But, the volume of songs got him a publishing deal and headed him in the right direction. His most recent album, *On The Road,* is his third for Arista Records and contains six songs that he co-wrote while touring. "The title is definitely apropos," says Lee Roy, "since the album was literally made 'on the road.' From beginning to end, from the birth of the songs to the final mixes, we never stopped touring. This was a new way of doing things for me." His first album, released in 1990, was only a minor success but his second album, *Love Without Mercy,* generated four Top 10 singles.

I CRAVE CHICKEN FRIED STEAK WHEN I'M ON THE ROAD

1 – 2 lbs cube or round steak cutlet
2 cups flour
4 eggs

1 tsp. each salt and pepper
½ – ¾ cup vegetable oil
¼ cup milk

In a large bowl beat 4 eggs, ¼ cup milk, 1 tsp of salt and 1 tsp of pepper. Set aside. On wax paper, sprinkle ¾ cup flour. Dredge both sides of the meat in the flour, then dip into the egg mixture. Dip meat into the flour once again until well coated. Heat ½ – ¾ cup of vegetable oil in a large frying pan over medium heat. (Oil should be ¼" deep in the pan.) Do not allow the oil to get so hot that it "smokes." Place cutlets in the oil, allowing their edges to get golden brown, then turn over. Once both sides are golden brown, reduce heat and cover pan. Cook meat an additional 15 minutes. (Keep cutlets in a warm oven until ready to serve.) Serve with mashed potatoes and gravy.

PEARL RIVER

The real beginning of Pearl River was in Mississippi, when high school students Jeff Stewart (lead vocals), Ken Fleming (drums) and Chuck Ethredge (guitar) formed a band called The Toys. They later added keyboardist/vocalist Bryan Culpepper and bassist Joe "Cat" Morgan. The Toys took home First Place honors at the Mississippi-Alabama Battle of the Bands for three straight years, then after years of wowing regional audiences, they entered the Jimmie Rodgers Festival Talent Contest and won top prize.

Two things happened at that contest. First, they heard a young musician wailing on a guitar in the backstage area and went to check him out. Derek George had grown up listening to The Toys and had an amazing feel for the country and blues that they played. They signed him on. The second

thing that happened was that Marty Gamblin, a Glen Campbell Music executive, was in the audience. Marty had been responsible for helping Alan Jackson get his Nashville break and decided to bring this band to Music City.

The Toys took the new name of Pearl River for their new incarnation. (The Pearl River runs through Mississippi and there is a Pearl River community on the Choctaw reservation near Philadelphia.) Things started happening quickly when they got to Nashville. They were selected from hundreds of entries across the country to be one of twelve acts to perform at the Nashville Entertainment Association's Music City Music Event in 1992. Pearl River stole the show and attracted the attention of four major record labels. They signed with Liberty.

DOES SHE NEED ME OR MY PARMESAN MEAT LOAF?

1 loaf Italian bread
1 lb ground beef
½ onion, chopped
½ bell pepper, chopped

1 cup grated cheddar cheese
1 cup parmesan cheese
½ cup barbeque sauce

Cut and hull out top of bread; set aside. Cook beef, onions and peppers, add barbeque sauce, cheddar and parmesan cheeses and cook until melted. Put the meat mixture in hulled out bread, put top back on. Wrap in foil and cook at 350° for 30 minutes.

CHARLEY PRIDE

On May 1, 1993, Charley Pride became the first African American to be inducted into the Grand Ole Opry. He is, in fact, country music's first African-American star. For the past quarter century, he has been one of the Top 20 best-selling artists of all time with 36 number-one hit singles, 31 gold albums and four platinum albums. On RCA Records, he is second in sales only to Elvis Presley.

Charley Pride unofficially started his music career as a ballplayer in the Negro American League. He played for the Memphis Red Sox, and would sing and play guitar on the team bus between ballparks. After a tryout with the New York Mets, he

decided to return to his home in Montana via Nashville. In January 1966, his first single hit the airwaves. Within a short period of time, "The Snakes Crawl at Night" was climbing the charts with his second single, "Before I Met You," close behind.

Today, Charley and his wife Rozene (they've been married over 35 years and have three children) live in Dallas where Charley's business prowess equals his recording career. He is the major stockholder in the largest minority-owned bank in Texas, First Texas Bank, and his extensive real estate holdings include office buildings in Dallas and Nashville, a farm in Mississippi, a ranch in Texas, a home in Maui and the Charley Pride Theatre in Branson, Missouri. He continues to work out annually with baseball's Texas Rangers and when not touring or recording (his 51st album, *Pride! My 6 Latest & 6 Greatest* is currently available) he loves to play golf.

MAKE AN ANGEL SOME SWEET AND SOUR BAKED BEANS

8 bacon slices, pan fried until crisp, drained, crumbled
4 large onions, peeled and cut into rings
½ – 1 cup brown sugar
1 tsp dry mustard
½ tsp garlic powder (optional)
1 tsp salt

½ cup cider vinegar
2 (5 oz) cans dried lima beans, drained
1 (1 lb) can green lima beans, drained
1 (1 lb) can dark red kidney beans, drained
1 (1 lb 11 oz) can New England-style baked beans, do not drain

Place onion in skillet; add sugar, mustard, garlic powder, salt and vinegar. Cook 20 minutes, covered. Add onion mixture to beans. Add crumbled bacon. Pour into 3- quart casserole. Bake in moderate oven (350°) for 1 hour. (Use larger measure of sugar if you like beans on the sweet side)

Makes 12 servings.

133

RESTLESS HEART

Restless Heart began as a five-member group: John Dittrich (drums and vocals), Paul Gregg (guitar and vocals), Dave Innis (keyboards), Greg Jennings (guitar and vocals) and Larry Stewart (lead singer). They had eight number-one records (six of them consecutive), three gold albums (*Wheels* in 1986, *Big Dreams In A Small Town* in 1988 and *Fast Movin'*

Train in 1990). Then, in 1991 Larry left to pursue a solo career and Dave decided to leave the band in 1993. "It's no secret that when Larry left we auditioned for a new lead singer," John Dittrich remembers. "But no one quite fit. Then we started hearing a few whispers in the industry, things like, 'Without Larry Stewart, they're dead.' Well, that really clinched it! That's when we said, 'Damn the torpedoes, full speed ahead! We'll do this, win lose, or draw.' It really did cause us to reach deep down in ourselves and come up with something new."

The "new" Restless Heart's first album, *Big Iron Horses*, produced the hit singles, "When She Cries," "Mending Fences" and "We Got The Love." "When She Cries" (which featured drummer John Dittrich singing lead) was the first country single to reach number one on the pop charts since Kenny Rogers' "Lady" and earned the trio a Grammy nomination.

WHEN SHE CRIES WE MAKE HER SWEDISH MEATBALLS

1 lb ground beef
1 egg
2 medium onions, peeled and pureed
½ cup bread crumbs
½ cup club soda

1 tsp salt
1 tsp freshly ground black pepper
½ tsp curry powder
4 Tbsp oil or butter for frying

In a large mixing bowl combine all ingredients except oil or butter. Taste and adjust seasonings. Roll mixture into 1" balls. In a large frying pan, melt oil or butter over medium heat. Add as many meatballs as will fit easily in the pan and fry until golden brown. Repeat until all meatballs are cooked. Serve immediately. Makes approximately 24 meatballs.

135

JEANNIE C. RILEY

Jeannie C. Riley's single of "Harper Valley PTA" achieved the biggest one-week jump of any single record in history. Charted at number 81 initially in *Billboard*, the record jumped to the number-seven spot its second week, a 74-point leap that has never been equaled. When it reached number one on the pop charts on September 21, 1968, it topped the Beatles' "Hey Jude" and established Jeannie as one of the first country female vocalists to achieve cross-over status. The record sold over eight million copies, won her a Grammy and was the Country Music Association's Record of the Year.

Jeannie released three albums while recording for Plantation Records: *Harper Valley PTA, Yearbooks and Yesterdays* and *Jeannie*. She then made the move to MGM Records where she experienced three more successful albums: *Give Myself A Party, When Love Has Gone Away* and *Just Jeannie*.

While maintaining her success in the country music marketplace, gospel music has also been a special part of her career. She currently records for Playback Records where she has had several releases including *Here's Jeannie C.* and *Praise Him*. Her autobiography, *From Harper Valley To The Mountain Top*, was a bestseller published in hard cover by Chosen Books and in paperback by Ballantine Books.

Jeannie and her husband Mickey make their home in Franklin, Tennessee, a small town steeped in Civil War history and nestled in the rolling countryside just south of Nashville. She says, "It's a welcome small town retreat from the rigors of the 'Life of Riley' on the road!"

JEANNIE C.'S MEXICAN CASSEROLE (APPROVED BY THE HARPER VALLEY PTA)

1 lb lean ground beef
1 large onion, chopped
½ tsp salt
1 can enchilada sauce
1 cup cream of mushroom soup

1 (13 oz) can evaporated milk
1 can cream of chicken soup
½ cup green chiles, chopped
Doritos chips

Brown onion, meat and salt, then add remaining ingredients—except chips.

Place layer of Doritos in baking dish; add layer of meat mixture and continue to layer until ingredients are used up. Top with 1 cup of grated cheddar cheese. Bake at 350° until cheese is melted.

137

RAY STEVENS

Georgia native Ray Stevens was a keyboard whiz kid. In his early years he studied classical piano, then formed an R & B band while in high school (always incorporating his infectious brand of humor between sets). He started listening to the rockabilly sounds coming out of Memphis and made the move to rock and roll. As a teenager he worked as a disc jockey on weekends and concentrated on writing songs.

When his parents moved to Atlanta, Ray began taking his songs to publishers. Even though he landed a contract with a Capitol Records subsidiary, Ray continued his education. He studied for three years at Georgia State University, majoring in classical piano and music theory.

In 1962, he made the move to Nashville, and it didn't take long before he became a household name across America. "Jeremiah Peabody's Poly-Unsaturated Quick Dissolving Fast Action Pleasant Tasting Green and Purple Pills" launched Ray Stevens as a major figure in both pop and country music. That was fol-

lowed by his legendary "Ahab the Arab," which enjoyed a renewed popularity during Desert Storm. The list of his standard comedy recordings is endless, and explains why he has won *Music City News* Comedian of the Year Awards for the past eight years (1986–1993).

RAYMONE'S FAST ACTION PLEASANT TASTING BEANIE WIENIES

1 medium onion
1 medium green bell pepper
2 celery stalks (10" each)
½ lb ground beef

1 pkg wieners
1 large (55 oz) can baked beans
1 cup brown sugar
Tabasco (15 dashes or to taste)

Dice and sauté the onion, green pepper and celery in butter until the onions look slightly opaque. Transfer this mixture to a large pot and set aside. Crumble and brown ground beef, drain grease and transfer to pot. Drain baked beans, remove any pork fat and add beans to pot. Cut wieners into bite-sized pieces and add to pot. Stir in brown sugar. Add Tabasco. Heat thoroughly over low temperature and serve.

CLIFFIE STONE

During his fifty-year career, Cliffie Stone has produced over 14,000 TV and radio programs. He was the producer of *Hometown Jamboree* (which aired from 1946 - 1960), *The Molly Bee Show* and *The Tennessee Ernie Ford Show* for television as well as *Gene Autry's Melody Ranch*. *Hometown Jamboree* was a launching pad for artists such as Johnny Cash, Eddie Arnold, Jim Reeves, Johnny Horton, Merle Travis, Tex Ritter, Liberace, Lefty Frizzell, Tommy Sands, Johnny Bond, Freddie Hart and many others. He has also produced a string of TV specials and has appeared on numerous TV programs.

Cliffie has always worn many hats in the music business: bass player, master of ceremonies, singer, comedian, disc jockey, song- writer, music publisher, record producer, artist's manager (Tennessee Ernie Ford among others), and numerous executive positions at recording and publishing companies. He has served as vice president of the Country Music Association in Nashville, and, in Los Angeles, he is currently on the board of directors of the Academy of Country Music (previously, he served as its president and vice president).

In 1972, Cliffie received the Pioneer Award from the Academy of Country Music, and in 1979 he was inducted into the Country Music Disc Jockey Hall of Fame. In 1989, he received a star on the Hollywood Walk of Fame and was also inducted into the Country Music Hall of Fame that same year. Today, Cliffie lives in Canyon Country, California, with his wife Joan and stays busier than ever. He has recently written a best-selling book, titled *Everything You Always Wanted To Know About Songwriting But Didn't Know Who To Ask*. It has received rave reviews around the world.

FAT-FREE POTATO SUPREME SHOULD BE IN THE HALL OF FAME

8 – 10 large potatoes
1 (8 oz) pkg fat-free cream cheese
1 (8 oz) carton of fat-free sour cream
salt and pepper
chopped green onions

garlic powder, to taste (I boil several garlic
   cloves with the potatoes.)
fat-free grated cheddar cheese
paprika

Peel, boil and mash potatoes. Add cream cheese, sour cream and seasonings to taste. Put in a 9" x 13" greased dish. Sprinkle with grated cheddar cheese and paprika. Put in refrigerator for at least 24 hours. Take out and bake for 30 – 45 minutes at 350°.

141

SUE THOMPSON

Sue Thompson (born Eva Sue McKee) came into the world in Nevada, Missouri, and spent her childhood on her parent's farm. She remembers country music and western movies as two of her favorite pleasures. "My parents bought me a second hand guitar," Sue remembers, "and my Mom, who played piano, encouraged me in my music. Gene Autry was my idol, and I wanted to be a singing cowgirl!" She taught herself to play the guitar and dreamed of appearing on the Grand Ole Opry. (She eventually was signed for a number of engagements on Red Foley's portion of the Opry.)

Sue and her family left Missouri and moved to San Jose, California, and it was in nearby San Francisco that Sue got her first big break. She got a guest spot on KGO-TV's *Dude Martin's Hoffman Hayride.* Her appearance led to a contract with Mercury Records where she had several hits, but eventually signed with Hickory Records in Nashville. "I was looking around for a new record deal," Sue recalls. "It was through my friends Fred Rose and Boudleaux and Felice Bryant (the songwriters providing hit after hit for the Everly Brothers) that I signed with Hickory." There, she had a string of classic hits such as "Sad Movies" and "Norman" (both released in 1961), followed by "James (Hold The Ladder Steady)," "Paper Tiger" and "Big Mable Murphy."

In addition to performing her classic hits all over the world, Sue has appeared in musical comedy productions of *Annie Get Your Gun* (with the Anaheim Civic Light Opera) and *Calico.* She makes her home in Las Vegas, Nevada.

NORMAN'S FAVORITE BROILED SANDWICH (JAMES LIKES IT TOO)

2 slices wheatberry bread
2 tsp mayonnaise
alfalfa sprouts
2 raw mushrooms, sliced

avacado slices
2 large slices beefsteak tomato
grated Monterey Jack cheese
sesame seeds

Lightly toast wheatberry bread. Spread a light amount of mayonnaise (1 tsp) on each slice of toast. Cover with alfalfa sprouts, then the mushrooms, avacado slices and tomato. Sprinkle cheese and sesame seeds on top. Broil until the cheese is brown and bubbly and the sesame seeds are toasted.

PAM TILLIS

Pam Tillis made her first public performance at the age of eight, singing with her father Mel at the Grand Ole Opry. By the time she was a teenager, they did not always agree on musical matters. "He was always very pro-country," Pam recalls. "He wanted to take charge of my career, but I always rebelled. The songs he wanted me to cut were just terrible." Laughing, she adds, "In retrospect, I did the right thing, Daddy. I'm sorry."

In high school and college (University of Tennessee in Knoxville) Pam was attracted to those rock artists who were showing their country influences: Linda Ronstadt, the Eagles, Crosby, Stills, Nash and Young and Little Feat. In 1980, she signed a record deal with Warner Brothers where she recorded "a real eclectic album." In the meantime, she became one of the more in-demand session singers in Nashville. Before long,

she was offered a contract with Arista Records. The timing was perfect. Her tastes had turned more country, and country music had taken its own turn toward the sound she liked.

Her debut single on Arista, "Don't Tell Me What To Do," made Pam only the fourth female artist to reach number one with her first single. The year 1991 was a busy one for Pam, highlighted by award nominations from the Country Music Association, the Academy of Country Music and the American Music Awards.

DON'T TELL ME WHAT TO DO
OR HOW TO MAKE BOLICHI

3 lbs eye of round roast
salt
olive oil
1 onion, diced
1 green pepper, diced

1 bay leaf
2 cloves garlic
½ tsp ground cumin or comino
½ cup red wine vinegar
4 potatoes, peeled and chopped

Rub salt into the roast. Place the roaster pan on a burner on medium high. Put 2 Tbsp of olive oil in the pan. Place meat in the pan and allow it to brown on all sides (sear the meat). After the roast has browned on all sides, add enough water to the pan to almost cover the roast, leaving only ½" to 1" showing. Then add onion, green pepper, bay leaf, garlic and cumin. (The Cuban equivalent of this spice is comino—it has a little stronger flavor and is recommended if available.)

Boil the roast on low heat for 2 – 3 hours. When the liquid in the pan has reduced to half its original amount, add red wine vinegar, then boil for another 15 minutes or until the meat is tender to the fork. Remove the meat from the pan and allow to stand and cool. To the liquid remaining in the pan, add potatoes and boil until done. Slice meat into ¾" medallions. Serve with potatoes and broth.

BILLY WALKER

A regular at the Grand Ole Opry for over 30 years, Billy Walker has performed in every state in the United States as well as in Austria, England, Guam, Ireland, Scotland, Italy, Japan, Korea, Okinawa, Spain, Sweden, Switzerland, Germany, Holland and Norway.

Born in Ralls, Texas, Billy was one of eight children whose mother died when he was only four. He and two of his brothers were sent to a Methodist orphanage in Waco and Billy didn't rejoin the family until he was eleven. When he was thirteen, his dad gave him a dime to see a Gene Autry movie and that set the pattern for Billy's lifelong love of country music. With some money he earned plucking turkeys for his uncle, he bought an old guitar and a twenty-five-cent instruction book. He learned at least one new chord from every "picker" that came to town, and taught himself to sing and play well enough to win a radio talent contest in Clovis, New Mexico, while he was still in high school. The prizes were: three dollars, a chocolate cake and weekly unpaid

appearances on a fifteen-minute radio show. That turned out to be a real break, despite the fact that for two years he had to hitchhike the 180 miles between his home in Whiteface, Texas, and Clovis.

He signed his first recording contract in 1951, which started a list of over 100 sides, 32 Top 10 hits and six number-one records. He did a long stint with Red Foley's Ozark Jubilee before joining the Opry in 1960.

THE TALL TEXAN'S TEXAS CASSEROLE

3 lbs ground chuck (browned)
1 medium onion diced
½ small green pepper diced
salt & pepper

1 pkg elbow macaroni
2 cans diced tomatoes
1 tube jalapeño cheese

Cook first four ingredients until brown and let simmer. Boil water for 1 package elbow macaroni and cook according to directions on package. Drain, add tomatoes and simmer 10 minutes. Add meat mixture to macaroni and simmer for 30 minutes. Just before serving add jalapeño cheese and mix well. Great served with cornbread.

CAKES

BROTHER PHELPS

Brother Phelps are brothers Doug and Ricky Lee. While many of music's great brother duos found their magic while growing up singing together, Brother Phelps' story is a bit different. Doug Phelps learned to harmonize with his older (by seven years) brother through tapes that were sent home from the road. More than twenty years later, they finally became an official duo.

The brothers grew up in the small town of Cardwell, Missouri, on the Missouri-Arkansas border, right on the Mississippi River. Their father, "the original Brother Phelps," as they like to say, was a minister at an Assembly of God Church and played guitar. In fact, their aunts and uncles played music, their grandmother wrote a thousand gospel songs, and there were always instruments (guitars, mandolins, piano) around. Ironically, both boys took up bass. At seventeen, Ricky was out of the house and working as a musician, eventually moving to Arizona. That's when he started sending tapes home. "He came home for Christmas one year," remembers Doug. "I played the tapes; I had learned the songs verbatim, but sang harmony. Ricky was floored." Even with the discovery of and enthusiasm for each other's voices, they still went their separate musical ways. In the 80s, they came together to be a part of the Kentucky HeadHunters and enjoyed a debut success that included a multi-award winning, platinum-plus album. When it came time to make a third album, Doug and Ricky Lee decided to make a go of it on their own as Brother Phelps. Their debut album, *Let Go*, is on Asylum Records.

You Can't Let Go Of Dutch Baby Coffee Cake

4 eggs
1 cup milk

1 cup flour
½ stick butter

Preheat oven to 450°. Melt butter in cast iron skillet. Mix all ingredients together in a bowl. Pour into skillet. Bake at 450° for 20 minutes. Top with butter and powdered sugar, honey or jam, etc.

LACY J. DALTON

Early in her career, Lacy J. Dalton traveled as much as 300 days a year and was on CBS Records' "most active" list for several years. Since then, her schedule has settled down a bit—she's on the road about 115 days a year now. She prides herself on never canceling a show due to health reasons.

Lacy was born in Bloomsburg, Pennsylvania, into a family of music lovers. Her father played a variety of string instruments, sang and wrote songs; her mother played guitar and sang harmony; and her sister was a pianist. Lacy's early influences were the folk rock sounds of Bob Dylan and Joan Baez and she's always been a writer and artist who loved music with a message.

Since 1980, Lacy has recorded a total of fourteen albums including three "greatest hits" packages. Nine albums were recorded on CBS Records and her fifth album for Liberty Records is called, *The Best Of Lacy J. Dalton.* Nominated for Best Female Vocalist several times throughout her career, she won the Academy of Country Music's Best New Female Vocalist award in 1979. Willie Nelson presented her with a gold record for her duet with him on his *Half-Nelson* album. (She was the only female to appear on this record.) She also received a gold record from Hank Williams, Jr. for her support of his tour commemorating his fiftieth album (*Five-O*).

Lacy continues to record for Liberty Records, and performs regularly at Harrah's in Reno, The Desert Inn in Las Vegas and several other showrooms throughout Nevada.

MISS LACY'S "NOT ENOUGH TO GET YOU DRUNK" COUNTRY FAIR CAKE

1 cup pecans, coarsely chopped
1 (18.5 oz) box of Duncan Hines Deluxe
   Yellow Cake Mix
1 (3.75 oz) box of Jello Vanilla Pudding
   and Pie Filling

4 eggs
½ cup cold water
½ cup Wesson Oil
¼ cup of your best whiskey
¼ cup dark rum

Grease and flour a 12" bundt pan. Place chopped pecans in the bottom of the Bundt pan. Mix the rest of the ingredients together well. Pour batter over the nuts. Bake 50 minutes at 350°. NOTE!!! Do not over cook! Cook only until golden brown, making sure the inside is done. (Check with toothpick.) Cool. Invert on a pretty serving dish. Prick entire top of cake gently with a toothpick. Drizzle glaze evenly over top and sides! Allow cake to absorb glaze well.

GLAZE

¼ lb butter
¼ cup water
¾ cup sugar
¼ cup whiskey
¼ cup dark rum

Melt the butter in saucepan, do not brown. Stir in water and sugar. Boil 5 minutes, stirring constantly. Remove from heat. Stir in rum and whiskey. Garnish with sprigs of pine or holly for a "festive" look!

BILLY DEAN

In less than three years, Billy Dean has become one of the top writer/artists in the industry. In 1992, the Academy of Country Music named him Top New Male Vocalist, and his song "Somewhere In My Broken Heart" was named Song of the Year. That same year, he was a finalist for the Country Music Association's Horizon Award and a Grammy nominee in the category of Best Male Performance, Country.

Billy was attracted to music early. His father was an auto mechanic who moonlighted as a bandleader and always encouraged his son's musical talents. When Billy was eight years old he made his first public appearance playing guitar in his father's band, The Country Rock. By the time he was a teenager, he was composing songs and performing along the Gulf coast of Florida.

Following a year in college (on a basketball scholarship), Billy was entered in the Wrangler Star Search competition and became a national finalist. When he performed at Nashville's Grand Ole Opry during the finals, the judges encouraged him to stay in Music City and pursue a career. But Billy believed that road experience was his first priority, and he toured extensively before moving to Nashville. Once there, he found himself in demand as a jingle singer and backup vocalist for many established acts, and his songs were getting recorded by artists such as The Oak Ridge Boys, Les Taylor and Shelly West. He soon signed a publishing deal with EMI and a recording contract with Liberty/SBK, where his first single, "Only Here For A Little While," soared to number two and stayed on the charts for nineteen weeks.

WHIPPED POUNDCAKE WILL ONLY BE HERE FOR A LITTLE WHILE

½ lb butter (2 sticks)
1½ cups sugar
6 eggs

3 cups flour
½ pint whipped cream
1½ tsp vanilla

Cream butter and sugar. Add eggs, one at a time. Beating thoroughly after each addition, add flour and whipped cream alternately: ⅓ flour–½ whipped cream, ⅓ flour–½ whipped cream, ⅓ flour. Add vanilla extract. Pour in greased tube pan. Put in cold oven and bake at 300° for 1 hour. Do not open oven door. Test middle of cake with wooden pick while baking. If it needs more baking, turn pan and bake for 20 more minutes. Do not over cook.

ICING

1 stick margarine, melted
1 box confectioners sugar
1 tsp vanilla
a little milk
1 cup chopped nuts

Beat together margarine, sugar, vanilla and milk until smooth. Add nuts. Ice cake.

EMMYLOU HARRIS

Born in Birmingham, Alabama, Emmylou Harris grew up near Washington, D.C. As a college student in the late 60s, she sang with a local folk duo, eventually moving to Greenwich Village to make a stab at a professional music career. She began to draw attention on the club circuit in both New York and D.C. and in time was introduced to Gram Parsons, formerly of The Flying Burrito Brothers and a heralded pioneer in the burgeoning country-rock movement. Emmylou toured and recorded with Gram until his tragic death in 1973. "After he was gone, I wanted to carry on with what I thought he would have wanted me to do," says Emmylou, "trying eclectic things, but always coming back to that electric country base."

On her 1975 major-label debut album, *Pieces of the Sky*, Emmylou introduced her Hot Band, which over the years has included such world-class players as Albert Lee, Rodney Crowell and Hank DeVito. As Emmylou moved closer to the heart of country music, she enjoyed seven number-one and 27 Top 10 hits. In all, she has recorded 22 albums (including a pair of greatest hits packages) and earned six Grammies and eight gold albums. Her 1987 *Trio* album with Linda Ronstadt and Dolly Parton was a platinum-plus success. In 1992, she earned the highest honor a country artist can aspire to: She was inducted into the Grand Ole Opry.

LEMON POPPYSEED POUNDCAKE IS THE ANSWER TO A COWGIRL'S PRAYER

3 cups all-purpose flour
2 cups sugar
¼ cup poppyseeds
1 cup sweet cream butter, softened
1 cup buttermilk
4 eggs

½ tsp baking soda
½ tsp baking powder
½ tsp salt
4 tsp fresh grated lemon rind
½ tsp vanilla

Heat oven to 325°. In a large mixing bowl combine all cake ingredients. Beat at low speed, scraping bowl often, until all ingredients are moistened. Beat at high speed, scraping bowl often, until smooth (1 – 2 minutes). Pour into greased and floured 12-cup bundt pan or 10" tube pan. Bake for 55 – 65 minutes or until wooden pick inserted in center comes out clean. Cool 10 minutes, remove from pan. Cool completely.

GLAZE

1 cup powdered sugar
1 – 2 Tbsp fresh lemon juice

In a small bowl, stir together powdered sugar and lemon juice unti smooth. Drizzle over cooled cake.

ALAN JACKSON

Six years ago, Alan Jackson was an unknown. Today, he is the recipient of three Academy of Country Music awards, five Country Music Association awards, two American Music Awards and numerous songwriting awards from the likes of ASCAP, *Music City News* Country Songwriters, *Billboard* magazine and the Nashville Songwriters Association International. To date the sales of his three albums have exceeded 8.7 million units in only four years. His songs "Don't Rock The Jukebox," "Chattahoochee," "Here In The Real World," "She's Got The Rhythm And I Got The Blues" and "Midnight In Montgomery" (his haunting song about a visit to Hank Williams, Sr.'s grave) have become country classics. Each hit song has helped to propel him onto new levels of success in the field of country music. New milestones have been reached and surpassed: number-one hits, multi-platinum albums, number-one videos, singing with George Jones, co-writing songs with Randy Travis and an induction into the Grand Ole Opry. A lot of success in less than six years.

Alan Eugene Jackson was born in Newnan, Georgia. Today he lives in Brentwood, Tennessee, with his wife and two daughters. He travels with six band members, The Strayhorns, and a crew of 26 on board three buses with four tractor-trailers hauling over 39 tons of lighting and video equipment. When Alan isn't traveling and performing, he enjoys fishing and collecting and working on cars, motorcycles and boats.

SHE'S GOT THE RHYTHM AND I GOT THE CHOCOLATE POUNDCAKE

3 cups sifted flour
½ cup cocoa
1¼ cup sweet milk
6 eggs
½ tsp baking powder

3 cups sugar
½ cup Crisco
2 sticks margarine
2 tsp vanilla
¼ tsp salt

Cream sugar, Crisco and margarine until light and fluffy. Add eggs one at a time. Mix well after each addition. Gradually add dry ingredients alternately with milk: ⅓ dry, ½ milk, ⅓ dry, ½ milk, ⅓ dry. Add vanilla. Pour mixture into large greased and floured tube pan. Bake at 325° for 1½ hours.

CHOCOLATE ICING

½ cup butter-flavored Crisco
2 cups sugar
¼ cup cocoa
⅔ cup sweet milk
¼ tsp salt
1 tsp vanilla

Put all ingredients in a saucepan. Bring to a boil, stirring constantly. Boil 3 minutes. Will thicken quickly as it cools. Ice cake while icing is still warm. If it gets too thick before you can get it on the cake, add small amount of hot water.

LORETTA LYNN

Recently, Loretta Lynn was leaving a New York hotel when she literally bumped into Rod Stewart. "I've always liked his music," she reveals. "I generally like rock music—except when it gets too loud and you can't hear the words." Just as she was introducing herself to Rod (who had already recognized her as the "Coal Miner's Daughter") a camera-waving fan ran up. "No pictures, please," Rod Stewart said, to which the fan replied, "I don't want a picture of you, I want one of Loretta." And so saying, the happy interloper thrust her camera into Rod's hand, and he took the picture.

Loretta cut her first record, "I'm A Honky Tonk Girl," on the Zero label, while living on the West Coast in 1960. By 1967, her songs and her singing style had established a new assertive stance for women in country music. She won the Country Music Association's first Female Vocalist of the Year award that same year. In 1972, she became the first woman to receive the CMA's highest honor, Entertainer of the Year. She won the CMA's top vocalist honors two more times, won four consecutive Best Vocal Duo awards with Conway Twitty (1972–1975) and today is CMA's most nominated artist. The Academy of Country Music named her Artist of the Decade, and *Music City News* has presented her with its Living Legend Award. But through all the honors, through more than 30 years and more than 50 albums, she says: "I've come a long way from Butcher Holler, but my heart never left."

In 1993, Loretta was part of the renowned *Honky Tonk Angels* album with Dolly Parton and Tammy Wynette.

THE COAL MINER'S DAUGHTER'S GOOEY CAKE

1 box German chocolate cake mix
1 can sweetened condensed milk
1 jar butterscotch/caramel topping

1 cup Cool Whip
3 Heath/Skor candy bars, frozen

Bake cake according to package directions. While still warm, poke holes in cake with a wooden spoon handle about 1" apart, halfway into cake (not to bottom). Pour sweetened condensed milk into holes. Pour jar of topping over cake and refrigerate. Once cooled, top with Cool Whip and crushed candy bars. Refrigerate overnight before serving. (This is optional, but the cake will set up better and be firmer if refrigerated overnight.)

BARBARA MANDRELL

Born on December 25th in Houston, Texas, Barbara Mandrell was a natural performer and musician. She learned to read music before she could read the English language and as a pre-schooler made her first public appearance playing "Gospel Boogie" on the accordion at her uncle's church.

Her parents, Irby and Mary Mandrell, were important musical influences in Barbara's life. When she was just eleven, Irby took her from their California home to a music trade show in Chicago where she demonstrated musical instruments. By now she had not only mastered the accordion, but also the steel guitar and the saxophone. Convention guests Chet Atkins and Joe Maphis were impressed by the talented little girl and she was invited to join the "Joe Maphis Show" at the Showboat Hotel in Las Vegas. Then came concert tours with Johnny Cash, Patsy Cline, George Jones and June Carter and next the formation of The Mandrells (Barbara, Irby and Mary).

In 1969, she began recording, unveiling a "blue-eyed soul" style that established her as one of country music's most leg-

endary stars. She's had her own successful TV show and is the first artist ever to win the Country Music Association's Entertainer of the Year Award for two consecutive years. In 1990, she released her autobiography, *Get to the Heart: My Story*. Within four days it made the *New York Times* bestseller list.

Barbara has been married to Ken Dudney for over 25 years, and they have three children: Matthew, Jaime and Nathaniel.

BAKE A KNOBBY APPLE CAKE AND THERE'LL BE STANDING ROOM ONLY

3 Tbsp butter
1 cup flour
1 cup sugar
1 egg, beaten
½ tsp cinnamon
½ tsp nutmeg

½ tsp salt
1 tsp baking soda
3 cups apples, chopped
½ cup pecans, chopped
1 tsp vanilla

Cream butter and sugar; add egg and mix well. Stir the dry ingredients together and add to the creamed mixture. Stir in the chopped apples, nuts and vanilla. Pour into a greased 8" x 10" pan. Bake at 350° for 45 minutes.

While still warm, top with whipped cream or vanilla ice cream and serve.

163

ANNE MURRAY

Anne Murray grew up in Springhill, Nova Scotia, amidst five brothers, the only daughter of a country physician. Her mother was a nurse. She enjoyed pop and folk music while in high school and in 1964, when in college, she auditioned for the CBS TV show *Sing Along Jubilee*. She didn't get the job, since there were enough altos in the cast, but co-host and associate producer Bill Langstroth (her husband since 1975) tracked her down two years later and convinced her to join the show. She gave up her career as a physical education teacher and never looked back.

Her first album was released in 1968, and her first single, "Snowbird" (1970), took her to the concert stages of the world. Over the years she has amassed four Grammy Awards, more than 26 RPM and Juno Awards, sold in excess of 24 million records and starred in numerous TV specials (including the CBS Disney special *Anne Murray In Disney World*, with guests Julio Iglesias and Patti LaBelle). She has been inducted into Nashville's Walkway of Stars, has her own star on the Walk of Fame at Hollywood and Vine and in 1993 was inducted into the Canadian Juno Hall of Fame.

Anne was asked to sum up the high points of her full and prolific career. She said: "The first time I ever heard my voice on a record with strings (I almost cried); when I won the Grammy for 'You Needed Me' because I was in such elite company; all the Grammys and Junos; selling out Radio City Music Hall for three nights and opening in Vegas and seeing Frank Sinatra's marquee on the other side of the street."

YOU NEEDED ME AND MOM'S CHERRY CAKE

1½ cups butter
2 cups white sugar
4 eggs
1 tsp each vanilla, almond and lemon
    extract
1 cup milk

4 cups flour
1 tsp salt
2 tsp baking powder
2 cups (approx.) maraschino cherries,
    drained

Drain and dry cherries. Coat the cherries with 1 cup of flour. Set aside. Cream butter and sugar well. Add eggs one at a time. Mix well. Add the vanilla, almond and lemon extract. Add the remaining ingredients: 3 cups of flour, baking powder, salt and milk. Mix well. Lastly, add the cherries. Pour into greased and floured pan. Bake at 325° for 2 hours. ENJOY!

THE OAK RIDGE BOYS

The Oak Ridge Boys are: Duane Allen (a native of Taylortown, Texas), Joe Bonsall (born in Philadelphia, Pennsylvania), Steve Sanders (a native of Richland, Georgia) and Richard Sterban (who comes from Camden, New Jersey).

The recipients of five Grammy Awards, four Academy of Country Music Awards, four Country Music Association Awards and two American Music Awards, the Oak Ridge Boys span three decades of hits. With ten gold albums and three platinum albums to their credit, each member has a distinctive persona, as an individual as well as a singer. Duane finds a great deal of pleasure and relaxation driving one of his fifteen antique and collectible automobiles that are housed in a museum called Ace On Wheels. Joe is a sports nut—with a particular allegiance to his hometown baseball team, the Philadelphia Phillies. Steve veered into acting for awhile, starring in the Broadway musical *The Yearling* and in the film *Hurry Sundown*. Richard's primary interest outside the group is sports and he is a partner in the Nashville Sounds and Huntsville Stars minor league baseball teams.

The Oak Ridge Boys work up to 150 personal appearances each year. Their tours are comprised of some thirty men and women: nine performers, a road manager, security, light and sound technicians, stage manager and other crew. They travel in three customized Silver Eagle buses with two 18-wheelers to move over twenty tons of equipment. They have done Command Performances for King Gustaf of Sweden, Her Royal Highness Princess Caroline of Monaco, Her Royal Highness Princess Anne of Great Britain, President and Mrs. Jimmy Carter, President and Mrs. Ronald Reagan and President and Mrs. George Bush.

ELVIRA LOVES MY PUMPKIN ROLL

3 large eggs
1 cup granulated sugar
⅔ cup canned pumpkin
1 tsp grated lemon peel
½ cup sourdough starter
¾ cup and 2 Tbsp all-purpose flour
1 tsp baking powder
½ cup chopped walnuts or pecans

approx. 12 walnut or pecan halves
¼ tsp baking soda
¼ tsp salt
2 tsp pumpkin pie spice
½ cup powdered sugar
cream cheese filling (see directions)
whipped cream topping (see below)

Grease and flour a 15" x 10" jelly roll pan or baking sheet with raised edges; set aside. In a large bowl, beat eggs with electric mixer for 5 minutes or until thick. Gradually beat in sugar, pumpkin, lemon peel and sourdough starter; set aside. In medium bowl, stir together flour, baking powder, baking soda, salt and pumpkin pie spice. Beat into sourdough mixture until blended. Pour into prepared pan. Bake in oven preheated to 375° for 12 – 15 minutes or until surface springs back when touched with your fingers. Spread a dishcloth larger than the baking pan on a flat surface. Lightly sprinkle powdered sugar over cloth. Invert baked cake onto cloth. Remove pan. Cut ¼" from all sides of the cake. Discard cuttings.

WHIPPED CREAM TOPPING

1 pint whipping cream
2 Tbsp powdered sugar
1 tsp vanilla

In small bowl, whip cream with electric beater until soft peaks form. Beat in sugar and vanilla.

Fold ends of cloth over the ends and sides of the cake. Gently roll up cake and cloth. Place seam side down on a wire rack. Cool to room temperature. Gently unroll cooled cake. Over cake, spread cream cheese filling prepared as follows: Combine 6 oz cream cheese with ¼ cup butter; stir in ½ tsp vanilla and sifted powdered sugar to taste. Sprinkle with chopped nuts. Carefully roll-up filled cake, removing towel as you roll. Place seam side down on a serving plate. Pipe whipped cream topping in swirls along top of roll. Arrange pecan or walnut halves on top of piped topping. Refrigerate for at least 30 minutes before cutting.

SAWYER BROWN

The five gentlemen who make up the group Sawyer Brown are: Robert Duncan Cameron, Jr. ("Duncan"), Steven Gregg Hubbard ("Hobie"), Mark Anthony Miller, James Thomas Scholten ("Jim") and Joseph Smyth II ("Curly"). The band got its start at the University of Central Florida, where lead singer Mark and keyboard player Hobie teamed up to pursue music. They moved to Nashville in 1981 and put together a band with bassist Jim, drummer Curly and, ultimately, guitarist Duncan.

They became the first band ever to win the Country Music Association's prestigious Horizon Award and quickly became one of country music's hottest concert draws, performing up to 220 concerts each year. In 1991, their song "The Walk" was one of *Radio and Records'* Top 10 songs of the year.

Duncan Cameron was born on July 27th in Utica, New York. He's single and enjoys flying antique planes. Hobie Hubbard loves pizza and going to the movies. He was born on October 4th in Orlando, Florida, and is also single. Lead singer Mark Miller is married, enjoys all sports and was born in Dayton, Ohio, on October 25th. Jim Scholten is also married. The Bay City, Michigan, native celebrates his birthday on April 18th and his hobbies are gardening and water skiing. Curly Smyth was born on September 6th in Portland, Maine. He is single, likes to read and enjoys outdoor sports.

DIRT CAKE
IS WORTH THE WALK TO THE KITCHEN

1 large pkg Oreo cookies
2 sticks butter
1 large pkg vanilla instant pudding
3 cups milk

1 cup powdered sugar
16 oz soft cream cheese
1 large container of Cool Whip

Crush cookies. Mix 1 stick butter with crushed cookies. Set aside. Mix the 3 cups of milk with the vanilla pudding. Set aside. Mix all the following together: powdered sugar, cream cheese, 1 stick butter and Cool Whip. Put this in a large container or make this cake look more decorative or realistic by putting it in a clean plastic or clay flower pot. First start with a layer of cookies and butter, then a layer of vanilla pudding and milk, then a layer of the cream cheese mixture. Keep repeating in this order until all of the mixtures are used up, saving some of the cookie crumbs to layer on top so it will look like dirt. Freeze overnight.

MARTY STUART

When Marty Stuart was only thirteen years old, he was on the road with the Lester Flatts Band, startling even veteran pickers with his world-class performances. As a young teenager performing on the Grand Ole Opry, he had no idea that twenty years later he'd be inducted as a member.

When Lester Flatt died in 1979, Marty branched out, playing a kind of bluegrass fusion with fiddle player Vasser Clements and working with acoustic guitar virtuoso

Doc Watson. He also began a six-year stint touring and recording with Johnny Cash.

Marty produced his first solo album in 1982, *Busy Bee Cafe*. The session band on the half-vocal, half-instrumental album attested to his industry respect. Doc Watson, Merle Watson and Johnny Cash on guitars, Jerry Douglas on dobro and Carl Jackson on banjo. In 1986 he made his major label debut on CBS.

Marty Stuart is a gold-selling, Grammy and Country Music Association award-winning performer and a BMI award-winning writer. Today when he performs, he plays country-rock pioneer Clarence White's 1954 Telecaster and a Martin D-45 formerly owned by Hank Williams. He also plays a D-28 that belonged to Lester Flatt. His new touring bus is a lovingly recreated and updated version of Ernest Tubb's old bus—where Marty spent many an hour learning how to play poker from the masters.

Marty visits his folks each Christmas, and his mother always makes his favorite—Applesauce Cake. He tells us it just wouldn't be Christmas without it!

APPLESAUCE CAKE FROM THE BUSY BEE CAFE

2 cups apples, cooked to applesauce consistency, or chunky applesauce
2 cups sugar
2 sticks of margarine, melted and cooled
1 cup pecans, broken in pieces
1 box seedless raisins

4 tsp baking soda
1 tsp ground cinnamon
1 tsp ground cloves
1 tsp ground nutmeg
4 cups all-purpose flour

Mix all dry ingredients; add raisins and pecans. Add margarine and applesauce. Mix well with a large spoon. Bake in a bundt pan that has been prepared in the following manner: butter bottom of pan, line with wax paper and butter again. Bake approximately 3 hours at 275°.

DOUG SUPERNAW

Doug Supernaw was born in Bryan, Texas, and moved with his family to Houston when he was five. His father is an Oklahoma-born Texaco research scientist and classical music buff, his mother an Illinois coal miner's daughter and lifelong country music fan. The mix of influences, Doug says, have led him to term himself "a sophisticated redneck."

He began writing songs when he was in high school, where his passion for golf got him a scholarship to the University of St. Thomas and led him to try out briefly for the pro tour. But college ended up serving mainly as a place to further develop his songwriting skills. "My economics class was good for about twenty songs," he says. "I sat right in the front row and they thought I was taking notes."

For four years he struggled in Music City, looking for his singing break while he worked as a staff songwriter for a local publishing company. In one of those strange twists of fate that so often accompany the most

compelling success stories, Doug Supernaw didn't start getting the attention that led to his breakthrough until he left Nashville. He headed back to Texas and put together a band called Texas Steel. They quickly became one of the hottest dance bands around, and soon he'd caught the attention of Nashville record companies. His first album, *Red and Rio Grande*, was released on BNA Records.

I'M A HONKY TONKIN' FOOL FOR LAYERED CHOCOLATE CAKE

1½ cups milk
4 squares unsweetened chocolate
1½ cups sugar
½ cup butter
1 tsp vanilla extract

2 eggs
2 cups sifted all-purpose flour
¾ tsp salt
1 tsp baking soda
1 recipe Special Chocolate Icing (see below)

Line bottom of 13" x 8" x 2" baking pan with waxed paper; grease and flour the waxed paper. Place 1 cup milk, chocolate and ½ cup sugar in top of a double boiler. Place over boiling water; cook, stirring constantly, until chocolate is melted. Remove from boiling water; cool. Cream the butter and remaining sugar in large mixing bowl with electric mixer. Add vanilla and eggs; beat well. Beat in chocolate mixture. Sift flour with salt; add to chocolate mixture alternately with remaining milk. Beat 2 minutes at medium speed. Dissolve soda in 3 Tbsp boiling water. Add to batter; beat 1 minute. Pour into prepared pan. Bake at 350° for 30 – 35 minutes or until cake tests done. Cool in pan 10 minutes. Remove from pan; cool on rack. Trim edges from cake; cut cake crosswise into 3 equal portions. Ice cake with Special Chocolate Icing.

SPECIAL CHOCOLATE ICING

½ cup light corn syrup
6 Tbsp water
5 Tbsp butter
1 (12 oz) pkg semisweet chocolate bits

Combine corn syrup, water and butter in saucepan. Bring to rapid boil, stirring until butter is melted. Remove from heat; add chocolate. Stir until chocolate is completely melted. Cook to room temperature before pouring over cake; chill until set.

173

CLAY WALKER

When Clay Walker was a senior in high school, he was faced with a tremendous dilemma: go to the prom or take a job performing for tips in a small restaurant. He decided to play the gig, where he was spotted by a local club manager who asked him to audition. At the audition, he played to a woman washing dishes and moved her to tears with a song he'd written. She then told Clay that she slept with the club owner and had some pull—she was the wife of his idol, George Jones. Eventually the club closed down, George Jones moved to Nashville, and Clay, then seventeen, hit the road playing gigs all over Texas, Arkansas, Oklahoma and Louisiana.

Eventually, he wound up landing a house job at Beaumont's famed Neon Armadillo. While there, he caught the ear of Clint Black's producer, James Stroud, and a deal was soon made with Giant Records. His debut album came forth with the number-one single "What's It to You?"

A native of Beaumont, Texas, and the eldest of five children, Clay knew he would be a singer after his father gave him his first guitar lesson at the age of nine. "My dad is an amazing guitarist, but playing has always taken a back seat to raising a family and working a ranch." Today, Clay still resides in his hometown of Beaumont with his wife, Lori, where he enjoys raising, racing and showing quarter horses.

WHAT'S MY CARROT CAKE TO YOU?

2 cups sugar
¾ cup oil
4 eggs
2 cups flour
2 tsp baking powder

1½ tsp baking soda
1 tsp salt
2 tsp cinnamon
3 cups grated carrots
½ cup chopped pecans

Cream sugar and oil. Add eggs. Beat well. Sift together dry ingredients and add to sugar mixture. Fold in carrots and pecans.

Pour into 2 round 9" greased and floured cake pans. Bake at 300° for 35 minutes. Makes 2 layers.

CREAM CHEESE ICING

1 stick margarine
8 oz cream cheese
1 tsp vanilla

1 lb powdered sugar
1 cup finely chopped pecans

Cream together margarine and cream cheese. Add vanilla. Beat in powdered sugar. Fold in pecans. Spread generously between layers, then on sides and top. Nutritional value—"What's It to You?"

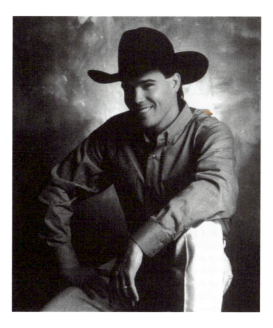

PIES

EDDY ARNOLD

Eddy Arnold has been making records and breaking records for over 50 years. In 1970, RCA presented him with an award to commemorate his selling over 60 million records. The total is now over 85 million.

Born in Henderson, Tennessee, Eddy grew up on a farm. He was brought up listening to the blues and mountain music of the area. His mother taught him how to play the guitar, and when he wasn't working the farm he'd listen to records and practice the guitar and the harmonica. He can't remember when he decided to become a singer.

Eddy Arnold is called the "Ambassador of Country Music," and his early recordings inaugurated the Nashville recording industry. He was the first country star with a network TV show and in 1966 was elected to the Country Music Hall of Fame. The following year he was the first recipient of the Country Music Association's Entertainer of the Year award. He received the Pioneer Award from the Academy of Country Music in May 1984.

Eddy resides in his native Tennessee, just outside of Nashville, with his wife Sally. The respect accorded him by his fellow Tennesseeans is reflected in the fact that both major political parties have asked him to run for governor of the state. But Eddy plans to stick to singing. He says, "If I won, I wouldn't have time to sing anymore—and that just wouldn't be me."

EDDY'S COCONUT CREAM PIE WILL MAKE THE WORLD GO AWAY

⅔ cup sugar
½ tsp salt
2½ tsp cornstarch
1 Tbsp flour
3 cups milk

3 egg yolks, beaten
1 Tbsp butter
1½ tsp vanilla
¾ cup moist shredded coconut

Mix sugar, salt, cornstarch and flour in a saucepan. Stir in milk gradually; cook over moderate heat, stirring constantly until mixture thickens and boils. Boil 1 minute.

Remove from heat. Slowly blend in beaten egg yolks. Cook another minute, remove from heat. Blend in last ingredients. Pour in baked 9" fluted pastry shell.

MERINGUE

3 egg whites
¼ tsp cream of tartar
6 Tbsp sugar
½ tsp vanilla

Beat egg whites with cream of tartar until frothy. Gradually beat in sugar, a little at a time. Continue beating until stiff and glossy. Pile onto pie filling; sprinkle on some coconut. Bake at 400° for 8 – 10 minutes, until brown.

179

GENE AUTRY

Gene Autry's career has spanned more than 60 years in the entertainment industry, a career that has encompassed every facet of the business, from radio and recording artist to motion picture star, TV star, broadcast executive and major league baseball owner. He is the only entertainer to have five stars on Hollywood's Walk of Fame, one each for radio, records, movies, television and live theatrical, including rodeo performances. He has been inducted into the National Cowboy Hall of Fame, has received the Songwriters Guild Life Achievement Award and the Hubert H. Humphrey Humanitarian of the Year Award.

Gene Autry has appeared in 94 feature films and has made 635 recordings. His records have sold over 50 million copies and he has more than a dozen gold records, including the first record ever certified gold for over a million copies sold, for "That Silver-Haired Daddy of Mine." His song "Rudolph the Rednosed Reindeer" is the second all-time best-selling single, boasting well over 25 million in sales. His recordings are on CD and cassettes and continue to be top sellers every year.

Today, he is the proud owner of the American League California Angels and the acclaimed Gene Autry Heritage Museum in Los Angeles. In 1993, his "Back in the Saddle" theme song recording was a part of the soundtrack for the film *Sleepless In Seattle*. The soundtrack album was number one on the charts for several weeks.

THE SILVER HAIRED DADDY'S PEANUT BUTTER PIE

1 cup peanut butter
1 (8 oz) pkg cream cheese
1 cup sugar
2 Tbsp melted butter

1 cup whipping cream, whipped
1 Tbsp vanilla
1 graham cracker pie crust
hot fudge sauce

Cream together peanut butter, cream cheese and sugar. Stir in the butter, whipped cream and vanilla. Mix well and pour into the graham cracker crust. Chill 4 – 5 hours or until very well set. Top with melted, thinned hot fudge sauce. Chill again for 30 minutes.

181

MARTY BROWN

Marty Brown still lives in his hometown of Maceo, Kentucky. He grew up in a house with all kinds of music; his two older brothers liked rock and roll and his three younger sisters liked disco and pop. But Marty liked the music his parents liked, and they had always dreamed of being country stars. "I cut my teeth on Hank Williams' music," Marty says.

While Marty was still in high school, he began writing songs and dreamed of going to Nashville. And he got there any way he could—hitchhiking or driving—knowing he didn't have enough gas money to get back home. He would spend his days there trying to get someone to listen. Finally, a featured segment on the network news show *48 Hours* opened a door for him. He signed with MCA and recorded his first album, *High And Dry*. "We shot a video in Maceo," Marty recalls. "All the marketing people started calling up wanting to know what the angle was. It was just me, just being proud of my hometown. With me there just ain't no angle. I'm just being myself."

Marty's second album was *Blue Kentucky Skies*, and he felt much more confident with the recording process. "Before the first album, I'd been recording at home. Then all of a sudden here I am going into these big studios with knobs that look like an airplane control booth. I was really in awe. I was going around and getting the bandmember's autographs. On the second album, I knew what it was all about." *Cryin', Lovin', Leavin'* is Marty's third album for MCA.

WILD KENTUCKY CHEESECAKE

2 pkgs Pillsbury crescent rolls
11 oz (1 8-oz and 1 3-oz pkg) cream cheese
1 egg, separated

1 tsp vanilla
1⅛ cups sugar: 1 cup and 2 Tbsp
¼ cup nuts (pecans or walnuts)

Spread one package of crescent rolls onto the bottom of an ungreased 9" x 13" pan. Pinch separtions in dough together. Pre-bake the bottom crust for 5 – 10 minutes first, before adding cream cheese mixture, just to make sure it gets cooked and doesn't end up too gooey in the center. In large mixing bowl, whip together softened cream cheese, egg yolk, vanilla and 1 cup sugar until light and fluffy. Top with remaining package crescent rolls—dough pinched together. If desired you can spread one can of pie filing on top of cream cheese layer before adding top crust. Cherry and blueberry are very good. With a whisk or fork, lightly whip egg white and spread on top layer of dough. Sprinkle with a mixture made up of remaining ⅛ cup sugar and nut pieces. Bake at 350° covered with foil for 20 – 25 minutes; uncover and let brown for 15 – 20 minutes.

FREDDY FENDER

Freddy Fender was born Baldemar Huerta in a poor Hispanic neighborhood in the Rio Grande Valley town of San Benito, Texas. The first music he played was "Tex-Mex"—the rambunctious combination of polka (from the German settlers in Texas) and traditional Mexican music. His parents were migrant workers and he traveled with them during picking season. Many of his fellow workers were African American, and Freddy got a first-hand education in the blues. The music he heard in the fields would become an integral part of his own unique style.

Freddy has had three successful careers: A Hispanic pop star in the late 50s (Spanish versions of Elvis' "Don't Be Cruel" and Harry Belafonte's "Jamaica Farewell" went to number one in Mexico and South America); a country/pop star in the 70s ("Before The Next Teardrop Falls" was the first single to ever reach number one on *Billboard*'s pop and country charts at the same time); and a member of the Grammy award-winning Texas Tornados in the 90s. The 60s were not so great. His song "Wasted Days and Wasted Nights" became a national hit, but stardom was stolen when Freddy and his bass player were arrested and sent to prison for three years for possession of two marijuana cigarettes. In 1969, he returned to the Rio Grande Valley and worked full-time as a mechanic, enrolled at Del Mar College and played music only on the weekends.

Today, his role as vocalist/guitarist in the Tex-Mex supergroup Texas Tornados begins a new chapter in his amazing career that spans nearly four decades.

You Won't Waste A Taste Of Apple Pie

6 – 8 sour apples
½ – ¾ cup sugar, white or brown
¼ tsp grated nutmeg or cinnamon
¼ tsp salt

½ Tbsp butter
2 tsp lemon juice
a few gratings lemon rind

Line a pie plate with pastry. Pare, core and cut apples in eighths, put row around plate ½" from edge, and work toward center until plate is covered; then pile on remainder. Mix sugar, nutmeg, salt, lemon juice and grated rind, and sprinkle over apples. Dot over with butter. Wet edges of under-crust, cover with upper crust and press edges together. Prick several places with fork. To bake, set pie in bottom of hot oven (450°) for 10 minutes. Then move to middle shelf, reduce heat to moderate (350°) and bake 40 minutes or until done. If upper crust browns too quickly, cover with paper. Serve plain or with cream, whipped cream or ice cream.

LEE GREENWOOD

When he was ten years old, Lee Greenwood started honing his musical abilities on the saxophone. (Today he plays a total of ten instruments including woodwinds, piano, guitar, sax and keyboards.) With both parents being musicians, he was quick to acquire musical skills. Born and raised on a farm near Sacramento, California, Lee formed his first band, The Moonbeams, while still in high school. In an effort to respond to musical career opportunities that were beckoning, he turned down a music scholarship at the College of the Pacific, abandoned a promising professional baseball career and even skipped his own high school graduation ceremony to play in Reno, Nevada.

For years, the "Greenfelt Jungle" (Lee's reference to the Nevada lounge circuit) proved to be an invaluable experience. Then his friend Felix Cavaliere approached him about forming a new group. Lee declined, and Felix went on to form The Young Rascals, whose first recording, "Good Lovin'," became number one in the nation. Instead of wallowing in disappointment, Lee found inspiration from coming so close to success.

In 1978, he flew to Nashville and recorded, "It Turns Me Inside Out." The song stayed on the country charts for 22 weeks. Two years after his debut album, he was voted the Country Music Association's Male Vocalist of the Year. The next year he won that award again, as well as a Grammy for Best Country Vocal Performance. His first three albums achieved gold status, his Greatest Hits also went gold and he's now recorded a total of eighteen albums.

Lee currently resides in Nashville with his wife, Kimberly, and, when not touring, serves as president of Greenwood Music Publishing Company.

GOD BLESS THE U.S.A. AND MY IMPOSSIBLE PUMPKIN PIE

½ cup Bisquick baking mix
½ cup sugar
3 tsp pumpkin pie spice
1 tsp salt
1 (29 oz) can pumpkin

2 eggs
1 (12 oz) can evaporated milk
2 Tbsp melted margarine
2 tsp vanilla

Mix in bowl Bisquick, sugar, pumpkin pie spice and salt. Mix together in separate bowl, then add to Bisquick mixture, pumpkin, eggs, evaporated milk, margarine and vanilla. Mix well and pour into large pie plate sprayed with Pam. Bake 55 minutes in 350° oven. Serve cool.

PATTY LOVELESS

Patty Loveless was born in Pikeville, Kentucky. Her father died from black lung disease when she was a child, and with eight children around the house, she became a quiet dreamer. "I loved music," Patty recalls, "but I was so shy that when my mother would ask me to sing for company, I'd go out in the kitchen and sing 'How Far Is Heaven' real loud so they could hear me but I wouldn't have to look at them."

Music was a release, so Patty began writing songs. Encouraged by her brother, who started running her down to Nashville in her early teens, Patty's songs caught the ear of Porter Wagoner, who not only became a booster to the scrawny fourteen year old, but introduced her to Dolly Parton. "Imagine being a little bitty kid and getting to hang around the Opry and their TV show with them!" she remembers. "Why, Dolly used to take me into the bathroom at the Ryman and show me how to put on makeup. To this day, Dolly is what country music is to me. Of course I'd have to go back to school on Monday, so it was a pretty different way to grow up."

Patty landed her first publishing deal when she was fourteen, but then there were several years that showed her a lot about life's realities. Then a new wave of traditionalism swept country music, and her brother was back pitching. It wasn't long before she had a record deal. Since then, she has stood for the integrity of hard country music and has nominations for every imaginable award, plus winning two TNN/*Music City News* Awards, an Academy of Country Music and an American Music Award.

JAPANESE FRUIT PIE
IS ONLY WHAT I FEEL LIKE MAKING

2 eggs, separated
1 cup sugar
½ cup butter, melted and cooled
1 Tbsp vinegar
½ cup coconut

½ cup pecans
½ cup white raisins
9" pie crust
whipped cream, optional

Combine egg yolks, sugar, butter and vinegar. Add coconut, pecans and raisins. Beat egg whites until stiff. Fold into other mixture. Pour into pie crust. Bake at 325° for 50 – 60 minutes. Cool. Top with whipped cream.

JOHN MICHAEL MONTGOMERY

Born into a musical family, John Michael Montgomery faced his first audience when he was just six years old as a member of his parents' band. The family played together until John Michael was nineteen, when his parents divorced. His brother Eddie replaced his mother on drums and when his father decided to retire from music, John Michael took over as lead singer. By the late 80s, he was a popular solo act around Kentucky, and the word eventually reached Atlantic Records in Nashville about the talented, lanky, blue-eyed singer who was knocking 'em dead in Lexington. So, you might say that instead of going to Nashville—Nashville came to him.

His debut album, *Life's A Dance*, was a smash and made him the only first-year contender for the Country Music Association's esteemed Horizon Award. His second album, *Kickin' It Up*, reached number one almost immediately.

"I've been in love before," John Michael confides. "I know how good it feels when you're in love, and I know how it hurts when you fall out of love. The kind of love songs I like are the ones that make you feel good inside. They'll make you cry, but they're happy tears. I will always sing songs like that. If there's one thing that can be predicted in my career, it's that you can always look for those kinds of songs on my albums."

I Swear My Favorite Pumpkin Pie Makes Life A Dance

1 unbaked pastry shell
2 cups pumpkin (fresh not canned),
   cooked and pureed
1 cup light brown sugar
2 eggs, well beaten
½ tsp salt

¼ cup evaporated milk
2 Tbsp margarine, melted
2 Tbsp dark cooking molasses
1½ tsp pie spice or ¼ tsp nutmeg,
   ¼ tsp ginger & 1 tsp cinnamon

Heat oven to 450°. Combine all ingredients and blend well, pour into pastry shell. Bake at 450° for 10 minutes and reduce heat to 350° and bake for 30 mintes with the oven door ajar. Pie is done when inserted knife comes out clean.

Marie Osmond

As a member of such an immensely talented performing family, it was inevitable that the show business bug would bite Marie Osmond—and at an early age! Although her brothers were into barbershop (and eventually pop and rock), Marie loved country from the time she was six. The first country recording to really make an impression on a ten-year-old Marie was Lynn Anderson's hit, "Rose Garden." Marie says, "I recall turning to my mother and saying, 'See Mama, you don't have to have a southern accent to sing country music.'" Marie's first record, "Paper Roses," was released just a few days before her thirteenth birthday and shot to number one in the nation. It was the first time in country music history that a female artist reached the number-one chart position with a debut record.

It wasn't long before Marie hit the road as part of her brothers' show. Her first performance was an appearance with them before a sold-out crowd at New York's Madison Square Garden. Soon *The Donny and Marie Show* was born, and, at age fourteen, Marie became the youngest person ever to co-host a weekly TV variety series.

In the 80s, Marie returned to her first love: recording country music. She began racking up a string of hits including "Meet Me In Montana" with Dan Seals, which won the 1986 Country Music Association's Vocal Duo of the Year award.

MARIE'S KILLER CHEESECAKE IS A LITTLE BIT COUNTRY

Crust:
- 1 pkg graham crackers, crushed
- 3 Tbsp butter, melted
- 2 Tbsp sugar

Filling:
- 3 (8 oz) pkgs cream cheese, softened
- ¾ cup sugar
- 3 eggs
- 1 tsp vanilla

Topping:
- 1 8 oz tub sour cream
- 1 Tbsp sugar
- 1 tsp vanilla

To make the crust, add sugar and melted butter to cracker crumbs (I put the crackers in a large zip-lock bag and let the kids crush them with a can—they LOVE it!) and press crust into a cheesecake pan. Bake crust for 10 minutes at 350°.

For the filling, combine softened cream cheese and sugar in bowl. Add eggs one at a time and add vanilla. Add filling to baked crust and bake for one hour at 300°. Remove from oven and let sit for 10 minutes. Then top with sour cream mixture and refrigerate for at least 3 hours. Garnish with strawberries or fruit of your choice. ENJOY!

RANDY TRAVIS

While growing up in North Carolina, Randy Travis was not getting into trouble or singing. He occupied his time watching westerns, riding horses and learning gun tricks. His father trained horses for a living; Randy began riding at the same time he began walking, and he dreamed of one day appearing in a western movie.

Randy opened the floodgates for the

"new traditionalist movement" in country music. At a time when Nashville was fumbling for a pop-flavored identity (that didn't please pop or country fans) and number-one records were selling only 30,000 copies, along came Randy Travis. A storybook country superstar, he overcame a troubled past with the help of Lib Hatcher. She helped him out of legal problems, nurtured his talent in her own nightclub and became his manager. Today, she is also his wife. His first album, *Storms of Life*, went platinum within a year of its release. He received two Grammys, eight American Music Awards, four Country Music Association awards and People's Choice and World Music awards. His second album, *Always and Forever*, was number one for ten months.

His music success led to film and TV offers. He appeared as himself in the NBC series *Down Home*, and that was followed by two appearances on *Matlock*, whose star Andy Griffith is one of Randy's biggest heroes. He grew up watching *The Andy Griffith Show* and *Mayberry, R.F.D.*, and to this day continues to watch at least an episode or two a day.

RANDY'S FAVORITE SOUTHERN PECAN PIE, FOREVER AND EVER, AMEN

1 cup white Karo syrup
½ cup sugar
¼ tsp salt

4 eggs, beaten slightly
4 Tbsp butter, melted and cooled
1 cup chopped pecans

   Mix all together. Do not overbeat. Put in unbaked pie crust. Bake at 450° for 10 minutes; reduce to 300° for 45 – 50 minutes.

SWEETS

HOLLY DUNN

About fifteen years ago, Holly Dunn was in her junior year studying advertising at Abilene Christian University in west Texas—an appropriate place for a girl whose father (the source of inspiration for her 1986 Grammy nominated song, "Daddy's Hands") is a Church of Christ minister. (Her mother, Yvonne has

achieved national renown as a Texas landscape painter.) Immediately after graduation (with a degree in advertising and public relations, that is currently in "some dusty drawer"), she took off for Nashville to follow her dream of a career in music.

After working a number of "make-work" jobs: bookstore clerk, travel agent ("I was terrible at that," says Holly, "I think I lost several businessmen who are still out there") and waitressing, she got a job working for Charlie Monk at CBS Songs. It was one of those jobs that embodies the dichotomy of the struggling Nashville musician. "I was a receptionist at the office," recalls Holly, "as well as being a full-time staff songwriter." She wrote the Top 10 hit "I'm Not Through Loving You Yet" for Louise Mandrell, and her songwriting reputation began to gather momentum.

She soon signed with the new MTM label, and when the company got rolling in 1986, she had enough material (including "Daddy's Hands") for an album. Two more albums followed. These albums, in turn, yielded four number-one hits and ten Top 10 singles. The three-time Grammy-nominated Holly then moved to Warner Brothers in 1990, where by the time her third album was due she had amassed enough hits to justify the release of a two-volume "greatest hits" package.

You Can't Keep Daddy's Hands Off My Healthy Oatmeal Cookies

½ cup shortening
½ – ¾ cup honey
egg substitute, equivalent of 2 eggs
1 cup plus 2 Tbsp all-purpose flour
1 tsp baking powder
1 tsp cinnamon

¼ tsp salt
⅓ cup lowfat milk
1 tsp vanilla extract
3 cups oats
1 cup seedless raisins (optional)
1 Tbsp of grated orange or lemon peel

Cream shortening and honey thoroughly; beat in egg subsitute. Sift together flour, baking powder, cinnamon and salt. Add to creamed mixture alternately with the milk. Stir in vanilla. Add orange peel and oats. Drop by teaspoonfuls onto buttered cookie sheet. Bake at 375° for 10 – 12 minutes. Makes 4 dozen cookies.

DONNA FARGO

Like so many of her peers in country music, Donna Fargo started singing in church when she was a child. She also sang at home to entertain her father's (a North Carolina tobacco grower) friends. But it wasn't until she graduated from college and moved to California to teach school that she began writing songs. There she developed her talent and soon recorded an album on the Ramco label, titled *Would You Believe A Lifetime?* The album did well enough to encourage her to persist, although not well enough to allow her to leave her teaching position. "I was real slow to begin performing live," Donna remembers. "I was really shy, and just didn't know if I could do it. The first show I ever did was in San Bernardino with Ray Price. I remember I paid more for the outfit I wore than I made doing the show! And boy, was I scared!"

It was in 1972 that her life changed forever with the release of "The Happiest Girl In The Whole U.S.A." She received a Grammy for it, as well as awards from the Academy of Country Music, the Country Music Association, BMI and *Billboard* magazine—and that was just in the United States. The album went gold in Canada and double gold in Australia and New

Zealand. Finally, she decided she could quit her day job.

More hits followed: "Funny Face," "It Do Feel Good," "Somebody Special" and many more. In 1981, she made an impressive debut as a gospel artist with her album *Brotherly Love* on MCA/Songbird. Donna continues to write and perform all over the world.

HAYSTACKS FROM THE HAPPIEST GIRL IN THE KITCHEN

1 can chow mein noodles
1 large pkg butterscotch chips

1 small pkg Spanish peanuts

In a large skillet melt butterscotch chips over low heat. Stirring constantly add noodles and peanuts. Drop by spoonfuls onto wax paper. Store when cool.

VINCE GILL

Vince Gill grew up in Oklahoma playing bluegrass music. In high school, he played in The Mountain Smoke band, whose credits included opening a concert for the pop group Pure Prairie League. The summer after high school, Vince was seriously considering a career as a professional golfer when a call came from Louisville, Kentucky, and he went off to join The Bluegrass Alliance, a progressive bluegrass group. After a year, he left for Los Angeles where he accompanied a friend to an audition for Pure Prairie League just to see if they remembered him from his Mountain Smoke days. They not only remembered him, they offered him a job. He recorded three albums with the group and put them back on the charts with his lead vocal on "Let Me Love You Tonight."

Vince left Pure Prairie League to join Rodney Crowell's band. In 1984, he signed with RCA and moved to Nashville. Three albums on RCA yielded several Top 10 singles, but no career breakers. In 1989, he moved to MCA Records. His album *When I Call Your Name* represented a long-awaited victory.

Vince Gill is one of the most powerful creative forces in country music today. In 1992, he was the co-host of the Country Music Association Awards, and his own collection of honors includes five Grammys, six CMA awards, four Academy of Country Music awards and six from TNN/*Music City News*. These honors cover everything from Best Album to Best Song and Best Single to Best Instrumentalist and Best Male Vocalist.

I STILL BELIEVE IN EASY APPLE COBBLER

5 cups apples, peeled and sliced
¾ cup sugar
2 Tbsp all-purpose flour
½ tsp cinnamon

¼ tsp salt
¼ cup water
1 tsp vanilla
1 Tbsp butter

Topping:

½ cup all-purpose flour
½ cup sugar
½ tsp baking powder

¼ tsp salt
2 Tbsp butter
1 egg, slightly beaten

Combine apples, sugar, flour, cinnamon, salt, water and vanilla and mix gently. Spoon into lightly greased 9" x 9" baking pan. Dot with 1 Tbsp butter. Set aside. Combine flour, sugar, baking powder, salt, butter and egg. Mix well and spoon over apple mixture in 9 equal portions. Bake at 375°, 35 – 40 minutes. Serves 6.

MERLE HAGGARD

Before he was 21 years old, Merle Haggard was serving time in San Quentin Penitentiary for a bungled attempt at burglarizing a tavern. The three-year stretch included a stint in solitary confinement for making home brew. After his time in solitary, he became a model prisoner and was paroled in 1960. In 1972, California's then-Governor Ronald Reagan granted him a full pardon.

Although he made his stage debut at fifteen (sitting in on a Lefty Frizzell performance), it wasn't until after San Quentin that Merle joined a band as rhythm/bass guitarist and began to sing in the clubs around the area of Bakersfield, California. In 1963, he had his first Top 20 hit on *Billboard*'s country charts: "Sing A Sad Song." Since then, the country charts have been his second home. To date, he has written hundreds of songs, including the classics "Sing Me Back Home," "Okie From Muskogee" and "Silver Wings." Over 40 of his singles have reached the number-one position on the country charts and 56 of his songs have received BMI awards. He has received eighteen awards from the Academy of Country Music, six Country Music Association awards, eight awards from *Cashbox* and five *Music City News* honors. He has released over 65 albums, four of which have been certified gold. The Country Music Association has nominated him for awards 42 times—more than any other male country entertainer.

PEANUT BUTTER COOKIES FROM MUSKOGEE

½ cup butter
½ cup peanut butter
½ cup white sugar
½ cup brown sugar
1 egg, well beaten

1¼ cups sifted flour
1 tsp baking soda
½ tsp baking powder

Cream two butters together, add the two sugars gradually, creaming into the butters. Add egg. Sift flour, soda and baking powder then add to creamed mixture. Form into balls the size of walnuts, flatten with a fork, making criss-cross marking. Bake 10 – 12 minutes in moderate oven.

FAITH HILL

Faith Hill was born in Star, Mississippi, the youngest of three children. "The first time I ever sang publicly was in church when I was three years old. My mother said I held the hymnal upside down and sang as loud as I could. I suppose I'd say it's my mom's fault and blame her for me singing. She started paying me 25 cents to sing at family reunions. If it was a big reunion, it went up to 50 cents."

Faith moved to Nashville when she was nineteen. "Some friends packed my stuff in a small truck and followed my dad and me. When they were all leaving to go back to Star, my dad was in the back of the trailer. I can still see his face. He had tears in his eyes and said, 'Take care. I love you and we're behind you 100%.'"

When she began job hunting in Nashville, she noticed that interviewers would ask if she were a singer. "I would always say, 'Yeah! Do you know a band I can play with?' Before long I figured out they wanted to know so they wouldn't hire you. They wanted somebody devoted to the job. Then I applied for a receptionist job at a publishing company and when asked if I wanted to be a singer, I said, 'No, you don't want to hear me sing,' and I was hired." For over a year she kept her singing a secret, afraid of getting fired. Then she met songwriter Gary Burr, who took her under his wing, and before long things began to happen. Faith's first album was released on Warner Brothers Records and her first single, "Wild One," was a smash hit.

TAKE ANOTHER LITTLE PIECE OF MY PEACH COBBLER

6 – 8 large, very ripe, fresh peaches, peeled
  or 1 large can sliced peaches
1 stick margarine
1 cup self-rising flour

2 cups sugar
1 cup milk
vanilla ice cream

Pit, peel and slice the fresh peaches into thin slices. Put peaches in plastic bowl and pour 1 cup sugar over them. Stir well. Cover tightly and place in refrigerator for 2 hours. Place the stick of margarine in the bottom of a rectangular Pyrex baking dish. Put in the oven at 400° until margarine melts. In a separate bowl, mix flour, 1 cup of sugar and milk. Beat well with a wire whisk. Pour mixture over melted butter. Don't mix! Spoon peaches over batter mixture. If you are using canned peaches, add only a small amount of juice from can. Do not stir peaches into the batter. Bake at 400° until top becomes golden brown. The mixture will come up and around the peaches and turns golden brown. Serve hot with a scoop of vanilla ice cream!

SAMMY KERSHAW

Sammy Kershaw grew up in and around Kaplan, Louisiana. When he was eleven, his father died and his mother went to work as a waitress to support her four children. It was then that his grandfather bought him a little Western Auto Tel Star electric guitar, and he made his musical debut at a fourth-grade Christmas play.

When he was twelve, his mother arranged for him to go to work for a popular local musician, not only to develop the talent she saw, but to keep him out of trouble. For eight years, Sammy served as J.B. Perry's protege, doing everything from setting up equipment to singing on the show. "It was a great experience," Sammy remembers. "We got to open shows for just about all the Nashville stars, so I heard them sing and learned their songs. I remember opening a show for George Jones when I was thirteen or fourteen and I'd have to say he was my biggest influence."

By the late 80s, Sammy was married with three children, had "burned out" on the music scene and took a job as a remodeling supervisor for the Wal-Mart Corporation. "For two years I didn't pick up a guitar or sing a note," he recalls. Then one day, out of the blue, he got a call from an old Louisiana music business associate who'd set up shop in Nashville. He encouraged Sammy to send the tape that led to his contract with Mercury Records. In 1993 he was nominated for Country Music Association and Academy of Country Music awards, racked up four consecutive Top 10 hits and saw his second Mercury CD, *Haunted Heart*, certified gold.

Pralines Cadillac Style

1 cup light brown sugar
1 cup granulated sugar
½ cup evaporated milk
2 Tbsp corn syrup

2 Tbsp butter
1 tsp vanilla
1 cup pecans

In a saucepan, combine sugars, milk and corn syrup, mixing well. Place over medium heat and cook until it reaches 234° (soft ball stage) on a candy thermometer, stirring occasionally to prevent sticking. Remove from heat and add the butter. Mix and cool until lukewarm (110°); add vanilla and beat until creamy. Stir in pecans and then drop by the teaspoonful quickly onto waxed paper or a piece of marble. Allow the pralines to cool undisturbed until firm and sugared. Makes one dozen medium-sized pralines.

BRENDA LEE

Brenda Lee loves people and believes the hugs of chambermaids and kitchen help on the closing night of an engagement mean equally as much as a standing ovation from the audience. With her worldwide record sales currently scaling the 100 million mark, Brenda began her recording career in 1956 at the age of eleven. Before she was out of her teens, she had cut a phenomenal 256 recorded sides including classic million-sellers such as, "I'm Sorry," "All Alone Am I," "Rockin' Around the Christmas Tree," "Fool Number 1" and "Emotions," to name a few.

Tiny in stature only, Brenda Lee is one of America's most in-demand musical exports. She has performed in 52 foreign nations including a Royal Command Performance

for the Queen of England as well as similar concerts in Mexico and South America. In 1983, she was inducted into the Georgia Music Hall of Fame (she was born in Atlanta), and in 1984, the National Academy of Recording Arts & Sciences bestowed upon Brenda their coveted Governor's Award. The glittering presentation, held in Nashville, marked only the fourth time the award had ever been designated.

Brenda says, "I'm everybody's fan, because I truly respect and love the music industry and the people in it. I think that we're all starting to realize that we are a 'family' and a family with a lot of potential to do good for the world around us."

SPOTTED DOG PUDDING

*This apple bread pudding recipe got its name from the raisins
that appear, scattered like "spots" throughout.*

1 cup dark brown sugar, packed
½ cup water
4 cups toasted bread cubes
½ cup raisins
1 cup tart baking apples, peeled and thinly
    sliced
¼ cup melted butter or margarine

2 eggs
1½ cups milk
1 tsp ground cinnamon
¼ tsp ground nutmeg
½ cup (1 oz) grated cheddar cheese
    (optional)
1 quart non-fat frozen yogurt

Preheat oven to 350°. In a small saucepan, combine sugar and water. Boil over medium-high heat until thick and syrupy (approx. 5 minutes); set aside. In 8" square baking dish, layer half the bread cubes, syrup, raisins and apples. Repeat layering process with remaining bread, syrup, raisins and apples. Pour on butter; set aside. In medium bowl, combine eggs, milk, cinnamon and nutmeg. Pour over layered ingredients. Bake 35 – 40 minutes. During last 5 minutes sprinkle cheese if desired. Allow to cool 15 minutes. Cut into 9 servings, serve with a scoop of frozen yogurt.

LITTLE TEXAS

In its earliest incarnation, Little Texas was made up of lead singer/guitarist Tim Rushlow, guitarist/vocalist Dwayne O'Brien, guitarist/vocalist Porter Howell and bassist/vocalist Duane Propes. These four, while on the road, met keyboardist/vocalist Brady Seals and drummer Del Gray. The Little Texas sound was complete.

In 1989, they were picked up as a development group by Warner Brothers Records, and their first album, *First Time For Everything*, produced five hit singles. In June 1993, the group performed a passionate acappella version of the National Anthem at a Democratic Presidential fundraiser. Honored with the invitation to share the bill with other great performers (Kenny G and Whitney Houston), Little Texas was proud to play their Top 10 hit, "What Might Have Been," for President and Mrs. Clinton. They were also chosen to perform on the nationally televised 35th anniversary show of the Country Music Association. They've toured with Clint Black, Kenny Rogers and Dwight Yoakam and were tapped for the 1993 Budweiser Rock n' Country Tour with Travis Tritt and Trisha Yearwood. At the Budweiser Rock n' Country date outside Austin, Texas Governor Ann Richards made Little Texas Honorary World Ambassadors of the Great State of Texas.

In 1993, the Academy of Country Music nominated Little Texas for both Top New Vocal Group or Duo of the Year and Top Vocal Group of the Year.

BIG TIME DESSERT

4 oz melted butter
1 cup crushed pineapple, drained
1½ cup Waverly Club cracker crumbs

1 cup diced peaches, drained
1 cup brown sugar

This is a layered dessert. Grease a medium sized baking dish. Start layering with ½ cup cracker crumbs, followed by ½ cup brown sugar, ½ cup pineapple and ½ cup peaches. Repeat, ending with last ½ cup cracker crumbs, then drizzle butter over top. Cook 30 minutes at 350°.

This is a recipe we came across during our travels. We have eaten so many wonderful things, but sweets are kinda a downfall for all of us. We hope you enjoy this as much as we did.

IRLENE MANDRELL

For more than a decade, the Mandrell name has meant sold-out concerts, gold records and award after award. The Mandrell magic first surrounded Barbara, then Louise, then Irlene, the youngest of the three sisters.

Like her sister Louise, Irlene was a member of Barbara Mandrell's band, The Do-Rites, before turning sixteen. As the group's drummer, she had traveled the world extensively before she turned twenty. She still picks up her drum sticks every year when she is Louise's special guest on her annual Christmas tour throughout November and December.

Her successful drumming career has been a bit overshadowed, however. Her career as a model and an actress (she has guest starred on countless TV shows) has kept her incredibly busy. Her modeling assignments have ranged from a seductive bedtime girl for a mattress company, to a tomboy mechanic for an auto supply chain, to an all-American Sunday school student on a national Methodist publication. She was the exuberant "Go Bananas" girl for Cover Girl on posters, television and in *Glamour* magazine. Other endorsements include a tour for Shedd's Spread Country Crock Margarine, 9 West Footwear and a Swift's Premium Brown & Serve commercial with sisters Barbara and Louise. Irlene co-hosted the award-winning TV show, *Barbara Mandrell and the Mandrell Sisters*, and went on to spend seven consecutive seasons on the nationally syndicated *Hee Haw*, where she was a featured regular. In October 1989, she was inducted into the Walkway of the Stars at the Country Music Hall of Fame in Nashville.

YOU CAN'T BEAT MY BROWNIES

2 cups sugar
2 cups flour
1 cup margarine
1 cup water
4 Tbsp Hershey cocoa

½ cup buttermilk
2 eggs
1 tsp baking soda
1 tsp vanilla

Grease and flour a jellyroll pan. Combine sugar and flour in a mixing bowl. 1 pinch salt (if you desire). In a pan on stove, melt margarine with water and cocoa until mixture is boiling. Pour hot mixture over the flour mixture and beat well. Add buttermilk, eggs, soda and vanilla. Beat well. Bake for 20 minutes at 400°. Frost using icing recipe below.

FROSTING

½ cup margarine
4 Tbsp cocoa
6 Tbsp milk
1 lb sifted powdered sugar
1 tsp vanilla

Five minutes before brownies are done, start making icing. In same pan you used to cook mixture above, combine margarine, cocoa and milk. Cook about 4 or 5 minutes—until mixture is thick. Add the powdered sugar and vanilla. Beat well and pour over the hot brownies. Sprinkle with chopped nuts if desired.

LOUISE MANDRELL

Born in Corpus Christi, Texas, Louise Mandrell was a junior in high school when she became her sister Barbara's first full-time bass guitar player as one of the original Do-Rite band members. Before her sixteenth birthday, she had worked every major city in the United States and Canada, and in clubs and on military bases all over Europe.

While still a teenager, she became a fixture on the Grand Ole Opry with the Stu Phillips Show and toured and recorded with Merle Haggard. In 1980, she leaped into the national spotlight as one of the talented siblings on the NBC TV show, *Barbara Mandrell and the Mandrell Sisters*. Louise has gone on to experience a string of RCA hits (including a hit duet with Eric Carmen) and, to date, has released a total of six solo albums.

In pursuit of her writing skills, her first book, *The Mandrell Family Album* (a 90,000-word autobiography), was an immediate bestseller when released in July 1983. She has now completed a series of children's books, the *Holiday*

Adventure Series (a sixteen-book series explaining America's most important national holidays).

In her spare time Louise enjoys interior decorating, weight-lifting and aerobics. She loves snow skiing and playing cards and is proficient at shooting trap, skeet and sporting clays. She won Top Woman Celebrity Competitor in Trap, hitting 23 out of 25 clay targets in a field of 24 women while competing in the Charlton Heston Celebrity Shoot.

SOME OF MY BEST FRIENDS ARE PEANUT BUTTER JUMBOS

1½ cups butter
1½ cups peanut butter
1½ cups granulated sugar
1½ cups brown sugar
3 eggs

3 cups all-purpose flour
1½ tsp baking soda
1 pkg Reese's Peanut Butter Chips

Beat together butter, peanut butter and sugars until light and fluffy; blend in eggs. Combine flour and soda; blend into peanut butter mixture. Stir in chips. Drop dough by level ¼-cup measures onto greased cookie sheets 3" apart. Bake in 350° oven for 12 – 14 minutes. Cool cookies on sheet for 3 minutes, remove to wire rack until cool. Makes 3 dozen.

KATHY MATTEA

Kathy Mattea grew up in the small community of Cross Lanes, West Virginia. By the time she was in junior high school, she had become more and more drawn to music. "Four of us formed a little group," she remembers. "We'd play at assemblies and school talent shows. But it wasn't till high school that I sang alone. I began to do solos with the choir and in church and that was when I developed a concept of myself as someone with a good singing voice."

She decided at age nineteen to leave West Virginia University and go to Nashville to pursue a career in the music business. At first she made ends meet by working as a tour guide in the Country Music Hall of Fame and waitressing at TGI Friday's. Then a job singing demos landed her a recording contract with Mercury/PolyGram in 1983.

On Valentine's Day, 1988, Kathy married songwriter Jon Vezner in a small Nashville church. They had met once before Jon moved to Nashville from Minneapolis, but didn't get to know each other until Jon went to work for a publishing company with offices in the downstairs of an old house on Music Row. Kathy was living upstairs, and Jon and a friend came to the rescue one day when her car battery died. "The rest," Kathy says, "is history."

Over the course of her career, Kathy has received many awards, including a Grammy in 1991, the Country Music Association's Female Vocalist of the Year in 1989 and 1990, and the Academy of Country Music's Top Female Vocalist in 1989. She has released eight albums to date.

MAKE APRICOT DAINTIES AND YOU'LL WALK AWAY A WINNER

I got this recipe from my friend Marcia. It's been in her family for years.

3 cups flour
1 Tbsp sugar
½ tsp salt
1 cup Crisco
½ cup milk, cool to lukewarm
1 pkg yeast, softened

1 egg, slightly beaten
1 tsp vanilla
apricot jam, for filling
powdered sugar

Sift together flour, sugar and salt. Cut in Crisco till mixture resembles coarse crumbs. Scald the milk, then cool to lukewarm. Add softened yeast, egg and vanilla to milk. Add this mixture to the flour mixture. Form into a ball. Roll out quarter of dough (at a time) on a pastry cloth dusted with powdered sugar. (Be sure to use a rolling pin sock—it's nearly impossible to do without the sock.) Cut into 2" squares with a pizza cutter. Fill each with ½ tsp apricot jam. Fold ends of pastry together and pinch shut. Let stand 10 minutes on cookie sheet before baking. (You may want to buy foil cookie sheets. The jam tends to leak out of the pastry and is impossible to remove from regular cookie sheets.) Bake 10 – 15 minutes in a 350° oven.

BUCK OWENS

In 1979, Buck Owens decided he was through with the record business. Country music at that point, he concluded, was no longer his kind of music. So, he settled quietly into his business complex in Bakersfield, California, and turned his attention to less ephemeral enterprises. Imagine, then, his surprise when nine years later his old label, Capitol Records, came calling to court him back into the recording studio.

If there was an epiphany that revealed it was time for Buck to return, it was country music's fascination with its "new traditionalists," especially the brooding and yesterday-minded Dwight Yoakam. "I began to hear about this Dwight Yoakam," recalls Buck, "and of course I'd hear him on the radio. People would send me articles in which he talked more about me than he did about himself. I had never met him, yet he dedicated his first album to me." Then one day Dwight dropped by Buck's Bakersfield office. He was playing at a nearby fair and wanted Buck to play with him. "It was the first time I ever got up on stage with anybody. He knew a whole bunch of my songs, and we did a little medley." This led to Dwight and Buck performing a duet at the Country Music Association's 30th anniversary TV special.

Privately, Buck is nothing like the wide-grinning rube he played on television's long-running *Hee Haw*. Although he left the show in 1984, he did return to star in its 20th anniversary special.

Buck has re-formed The Buckaroos and is back on the road. With him it's all-or-nothing. "I don't think you can do it half-way—not if you love the music and the music loves you."

MOTHER OWENS' BANANA PUDDING

1 cup sugar
3 Tbsp flour
½ tsp salt
2 eggs

2½ cups milk
2 tsp vanilla
1 small box vanilla wafers
4 large bananas, sliced

Combine sugar, flour and salt. Add eggs to milk and mix. Add to sugar/flour/salt mixture and blend. Cook over medium heat, stirring constantly, until thickened. Add vanilla and remove from heat. Line bottom of bowl or pan with vanilla wafers, then a layer of sliced bananas over the wafers. Put part of the cooked custard over the layers. Repeat another set of layers of wafers and bananas, ending with custard mixture. Sprinkle with wafer crumbs. Refrigerate until well chilled.

"This is one of my all-time favorites. When I was growing up in Texas, Mother would fix up big batches of this for all us kids and we liked it so much that somehow what leftovers there were never did stay in the icebox too long. When she used to fix it for me when I grew up, I got very greedy with it and sometimes I just refused to share with anyone.

"Mother cooked with 'dibs, fingerfuls and just-a-bits,' so these amounts are as close as anybody can come to a recipe. I hope you enjoy it as much as my family always has."

221

DOLLY PARTON

Four-time Grammy award winner Dolly Rebecca Parton was born the fourth of twelve children to a hard-working farm couple in the impoverished East Tennessee hills. By the age of six, she was singing in her grandfather's church and at seven she started playing guitar. By the time she was ten years old, she was performing on the *Cass Walker Show* in Knoxville and made her first record when she was thirteen. The day after she graduated from high school in 1959, she left for Nashville. On her first afternoon there she met the man who would, two years later in May 1966, become her husband, Carl Dean.

Dolly's career took off after country music superstar Porter Wagoner began featuring her on his popular syndicated TV show. *The Porter Wagoner Show* would expose Dolly to over 45 million people in more than 100 markets and attract the attention of RCA Records. Dolly quickly blossomed into one of the best-selling country artists in music history.

In May 1986, Dolly saw one of her cherished dreams become reality. The opening of Dollywood, an entertainment theme park to preserve her Smoky Mountain heritage and East Tennessee lifestyle.

Dolly wrote the song "I Will Always Love You" in 1974, and it became a number-one record for her. Ten years later, she sang the song again in her second movie, *The Best Little Whorehouse in Texas*, and again it went to number one. Then, in 1992, Whitney Houston sang "I Will Always Love You" in her film *The Body Guard*. The song went to number one for the third time and sold in excess of four million records.

YOU WILL ALWAYS LOVE MY FAVORITE DESSERT

3 eggs, separated
⅔ cup sugar
2 heaping tsp flour
1 quart milk

1 tsp vanilla
nutmeg, optional

Cream egg yolks with sugar and whip until smooth, add flour and mix well. Scald the milk, and when hot enough, add the creamed mixture. Stir constantly, 20 – 25 minutes until it thickens, remove from heat and add vanilla. Boil some water. Whip egg whites and add to boiled water until hardened. Remove with spatula and put on top of the cream mixture. Sprinkle with nutmeg. Chill.

EDDIE RABBITT

Eddie Rabbitt was born in Brooklyn and raised in East Orange, New Jersey, the son of Irish immigrants. His father played the fiddle and accordion, and Eddie learned to play the guitar by the time he was twelve years old. In 1968, with $1,000 in his pocket and no music business contacts, he took a Greyhound bus to Nashville. He began writing songs in the hopes that an established star might record one. In 1970, he struck gold when Elvis's recording of his song "Kentucky Rain" established him as a songwriter. Today, he has more than twenty BMI songwriter awards in country music and more than a dozen in pop. Ten of his songs have achieved "million air" status, with more than one million radio plays each.

Eddie signed his first recording contract in 1974. His second album, *Rocky Mountain Music,* was a country hit that crossed over to the pop charts. In 1979, he had a hit with the theme from the Clint Eastwood movie, *Every Which Way But Loose.* His single "Suspicions" followed and won BMI's Robert J. Burton Award in 1980 as the most performed song of the year. He has continued to enjoy a string of hits including the smash duet with Crystal Gayle, "You And I." His seventeen albums have garnered 26 number-one country hits and eight Top 40 hits.

ON SECOND THOUGHT I'LL HAVE SOME MORE TORTONI MOLD

1 (14 oz) can Eagle brand sweetened
condensed milk (not evaporated milk)
3 egg yolks, beaten*
¼ cup light rum
2 tsp vanilla
⅔ cup coconut macaroon crumbs (about 5
large cookies)

½ – ¾ cup toasted slivered almonds
⅓ cup chopped maraschino cherries
2 cups (1 pint) whipping cream, whipped
Additional maraschino cherries, toasted
slivered almonds and mint leaves optional

In a large bowl, combine all ingredients except whipped cream, additional cherries, almonds and mint; mix well. Fold in whipped cream. Pour into lightly oiled 1½-quart mold; cover with aluminum foil. Freeze 6 hours or until firm. Using a hot cloth on outside of mold, unmold onto serving plate. Garnish with cherries, almonds and mint leaves if desired. Return leftovers to freezer.

*Use only Grade A clean, uncracked eggs.

T. G. SHEPPARD

T. G. Sheppard has always had a passion for music. In fact, he was a fifteen year old growing up in Humboldt, Tennessee, when he got the itch to run away to Memphis to begin his musical career. He gained invaluable experience performing at parties and in clubs under his given name, Bill Browder. It wasn't long before he started his own company and established himself as a full-time record promoter for various labels, including RCA. During this time he realized that singing was his first love and took the stage name of T. G. Sheppard.

In 1974, T. G. acquired a big break when his first single, "Devil In The Bottle," became a number-one hit song. Although he was beginning to "happen," he continued his promotion work and cultivated a close friendship with Elvis. The legendary performer appreciated T. G.'s unique style and personality and, as a token of their friendship, gave T. G. his first tour bus in 1976.

T. G.'s recording career began to skyrocket at Warner Brothers Records, where he enjoyed ten consecutive number-one hits. He later moved to Columbia Records, where he experienced three hit albums. Now signed to Curb Records, T. G. is working on his first album for the label, the 25th of his professional career.

One of T. G.'s weaknesses is his love of Mexican food. In 1989, he opened "T. G.'s North of the Border," a 200-seat authentic Mexican restaurant located in Gatlinburg, Tennessee. He is also an auto racing enthusiast and is often on hand to sing the national anthem at various NASCAR races.

EAT SUNRISE BREAD PUDDING
IF YOU WANNA GO TO HEAVEN

5 eggs
1 quart milk
3 cups sugar

1/ or 1bc.

dash of lemon flavoring
4 slices bread, crumbled
sugar and cinnamon

Beat eggs until fluffy; stir in milk. Add sugar and lemon flavoring, then crumbled bread. Pour mixture into a baking dish and sprinkle with sugar and cinnamon.

Bake at 350° to a custard consistency. Serve warm in the morning for breakfast, or refrigerate and serve cold as a mid afternoon snack!

RED STEAGALL

Over the past fifteen years, Red Steagall has performed an average of 200 days a year. He has toured Germany, Spain, Australia, the Middle East and South America, including over 100 major fair and rodeo appearances. Although Red is best known for his Texas swing dance music and such songs as "Here We Go Again," "Party Dolls And Wine," "Freckles Brown" and "Lone Star Beer And Bob Wills Music,"

Red is beloved by Texas cowboys for the quiet times they have spent with him around chuck wagon campfires. In their opinion, Red's best music has never been heard by the public.

A native of Texas, Red had a career in agricultural chemistry after graduating from West Texas State University. He then moved on to spend eight years as a music industry executive in Los Angeles, but finally found his niche as a recording artist, songwriter and television and motion picture personality (including a major role in the film *Benji The Hunted*). Red also produced the motion picture *Big Bad John*, starring Jimmy Dean, Jack Elam, Ned Beatty and Bo Hopkins. He has released a total of thirteen albums and has made numerous appearances on such syndicated TV shows as, *Nashville On The Road*, *Music Country U.S.A.* and *Hee Haw*.

In 1991, the Texas Legislature named Red as the official Cowboy Poet of Texas and in March 1993, Texas Christian University Press published his first book: *Ride For The Brand*. It is a collection of poetry and songs embracing the western lifestyle that Red loves and lives.

DAYBREAK DELIGHT AFTER A NIGHT OF LONE STAR BEER AND BOB WILLS MUSIC

Several years ago I purchased a chuck wagon and now take it with me to many of the places I perform. We offer the same types of foods that are served from a chuck wagon riding the trail including biscuits, barbeque beef, fried potatoes and so forth. Daybreak Delight is an unusual recipe that includes both canned and dry ingredients that are often carried on the trail.

2 cans pineapple tidbits
½ cup flour
½ cup sugar

2 cups grated cheese
crushed Ritz crackers
butter or margarine

Drain most of the juice and then layer pineapple tidbits into a 9" x 13" baking dish. Combine sugar and flour and sprinkle over the top. Then layer with grated cheese and finally with Ritz crackers. Dot with one stick of butter. Bake at 325° or cook over an open fire until bubbly in the center.

PORTER WAGONER

When Porter Wagoner's name is mentioned, images instantly emerge of the tall man with the big smile and the flashy costumes. Porter Wagoner is a country music star in the truest sense of the term.

Porter began his career when he was a young grocery store clerk. Sitting around playing guitar and singing during store hours would not appear to be a good way for an employee to remain in his boss's good graces, but it proved to be Porter's ticket into show business. When things were slow in the West Plains, Missouri, grocery store, he'd drag out his guitar and play for anyone who'd care to listen. The owner of the market enjoyed Porter's singing and decided to sponsor a fifteen-minute early-morning radio show to showcase the talent of his young clerk. This led to Porter's landing a weekly spot on KWTO radio in Springfield, and a few months later *Ozark Jubilee* with Red Foley came to the station. Red taught Porter many lessons of showmanship that were instrumental to his later success.

In 1955, he signed with RCA and began a recording career there that spanned over twenty years. In 1957, he was invited to join the Grand Ole Opry. His long-running TV series began in 1961, and in 1967 he auditioned a young singer who would become his singing partner—Dolly Parton—until 1974.

Today, Porter devotes his time to entertaining with The Wagonmasters. Occasionally, when his schedule gets too hectic, he heads "out to the lake" to get some rest. Rest for him consists of non-stop fishing.

FUDGE FOR A SATISFIED MIND

My mother taught me this when I was a boy and I've never forgotten it.

Mix in pan:

2 cups sugar
2 heaping Tbsp cocoa

½ tsp salt
¼ cup Log Cabin syrup

Add enough milk to make it soupy, but very thick. Bring to boil, and boil until sugar is dissolved, 4 – 5 minutes. Test by dropping into water until it forms a ball.

Remove from heat and add:

2 Tbsp butter
1 tsp vanilla

Stir until it begins to cool. Add:

2 Tbsp peanut butter
½ cup English walnuts

Pour into a large platter until it cools and hold a gun on yourself until you taste it!

STEVE WARINER

Steve Wariner has been making music since he was nine years old in Indiana. Born on Christmas Day, 1954, Steve was performing with his father, Roy, doing weekly radio and TV shows. When he was seventeen, he was discovered by Dottie West, who hired him as her bassist. Then came stints with Bob Luman and Chet Atkins before signing with RCA in 1977.

"I was so excited on the day of my first recording session," Steve recalls. "But there were all these network TV crews clamoring around to talk to Chet Atkins and the other Nashville studio pickers. It was the day after Elvis died. So there I was, just a kid, huddled back in the corner." He enjoyed five Top 10 hits at RCA, but it was at MCA Records (1984–1990) that he was consistently on country music's Top 10. His 1986 duet with Nicolette Larson, "That's How You Know When Love's Right," was nominated for a Country Music Association award. "The Hand That Rocks The Cradle," a 1987 duet with Glen Campbell, was nominated for a Grammy. In 1991, Steve collaborated with Mark O'Connor, Vince Gill and Ricky Skaggs on "Restless." Billed as The New Nashville Cats, they shared both a Grammy and a CMA award.

Today, Steve records for Arista and when he's not in the studio, writing or perform-ing, he loves to paint. When the kids are in bed and things are quiet, he goes off to his private studio and works in watercolors. Steve is also an accomplished magician, although he says he's "rusty." His specialty is "close up," not big stage, magic tricks. "That," he explains "is why I've never incorporated magic into my concert act."

ALL ROADS LEAD TO REFRIGERATOR COOKIES

1 cup shortening
1 cup sugar
1 cup brown sugar, firmly packed
2 eggs, well beaten
2 tsp vanilla

1½ cups sifted flour
1 tsp baking soda
½ tsp salt
3 cups quick cooking oats

Cream together shortening and sugars until light and fluffy. Add eggs one at a time, beating well after each addition. Blend in vanilla. Sift together flour, baking soda and salt. Gradually add dry ingredients to creamed mixture; mix well. Stir in oats. Divide dough in thirds. Shape in 10" x 1 ¼" rolls. Wrap tightly in plastic wrap or waxed paper. Chill several hours or overnight. Cut rolls in thin slices. Place about 1½" apart on ungreased baking sheets. Bake in 400° oven 6 – 8 minutes or until done. Remove from baking sheets. Cool on racks. Makes about 8 dozen.

MICHELLE WRIGHT

Michelle Wright grew up in Merlin, Ontario, a small Canadian farming community. "I was born and raised on country music," says Michelle, whose parents were both country performers. "It was all I ever listened to on the radio." But she also heard the rhythm and blues and Motown hits coming out of Detroit, just 45 minutes away.

Michelle began touring and playing clubs right out of high school, and by 1988 she had released her first album in Canada. "Success has been a twelve-year process in Canada," she says. "It took a long time for people to get to know me, but that experience really prepared me for the American audience." Recognizing the massive potential in her husky voice, Arista Records made Michelle the third artist signed when the label opened its country division in 1990. Her self-titled debut album paved the way for success in the United States and contributed to her being a mainstay at the Canadian awards shows, including a four-year reign as the Canadian Country Music Association's Female Vocalist of the Year—a title she still holds. She's since added the Academy of Country Music's Top New Female Vocalist award to her list of honors.

ANGEL COOKIES—TAKE 'EM LIKE A MAN

2 eggs
1 Tbsp sugar
1½ Tbsp heavy cream

approx. 1 cup all-purpose flour
powdered sugar

Beat the eggs until light and lemon colored; add cream and sugar. Add flour to make a stiff dough; cut in 2½" strips on a slant. Cut in 2½" strips in the other direction to make diamonds. Cut a slit in the middle; pull one corner through and out to twist the cookie. Fry in deep fat at 365° to brown; drain on paper towel. Shake on a generous amount of powdered sugar. Keep at room temperature.

TAMMY WYNNETTE

Tammy Wynette was born Virginia Wynette Pugh near Tupelo, Mississippi. She was raised in Alabama and grew up singing with her family and dreaming of making it in the music business. But a young marriage and children made her practical, and she began a career as a hairdresser. As for so many great artists, though, music's pull was too strong. She went to Nashville, was met with general indifference and was ready to leave when producer Billy Sherrill couldn't lease a master recording of "Apartment #9" and called the young woman who'd been in his office the day before to cut it for him. That was Tammy, and that was the beginning.

The team of Wynette and Sherrill helped define country music in the late 60s and 70s with an amazing string of hits including "D-I-V-O-R-C-E" and her classic "Stand By Your Man."

Tammy recently triumphed as a featured guest with The KLF on their dance smash "Justified and Ancient." It became a world-wide Top 10 hit and ranks as the highest-charting single featuring a country artist since

Kenny Rogers and Dolly Parton's "Islands in the Stream" duet topped the pop, country and contemporary charts. Her *Higher Ground* duet project, which paired her with Rodney Crowell, The O'Kanes, Vern Gosdin and Emmylou Harris, re-emphasized her country roots. Her duet on Randy Travis's *Heroes and Friends* project finds the pair almost recapturing the celebrated George Jones/Tammy Wynette magic.

STAND BY YOUR MAN AND MAKE HIM SOME OLD FASHIONED TEA CAKES

1½ cups margarine
3 eggs, beaten thoroughly
2 cups sugar

1 Tbsp vanilla
1 Tbsp baking powder
4 cups self-rising flour

Soften margarine to room temperature. Beat in eggs, sugar and vanilla. Add baking powder to flour and sift together slowly into margarine mixture. Roll out dough on floured board and cut with cookie cutter. Bake in preheated oven at 350° until as brown as desired. Makes 5 – 6 dozen.

ARTIST INDEX

Food Index

PHOTO CREDITS